The Late
Roman Empire

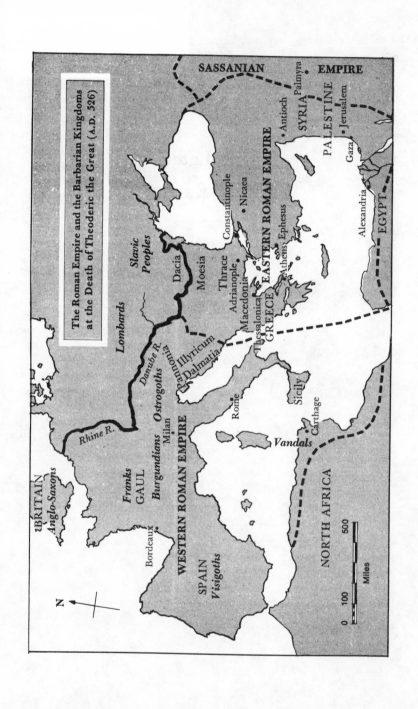

The Roman Empire and the Barbarian Kingdoms at the Death of Theoderic the Great (A.D. 526)

SASSANIAN EMPIRE

Palmyra

Antioch
SYRIA

Jerusalem
PALESTINE

Gaza

EGYPT

Alexandria

Constantinople
Nicaea

EASTERN ROMAN EMPIRE

Ephesus
Athens
GREECE

Thrace
Adrianople
Macedonia
Thessalonica

Moesia

Dacia

Slavic Peoples

Lombards

Danube R.
Pannonia
Ostrogoths
Illyricum
Dalmatia

Milan
Burgundians

Rhine R.

Franks
GAUL

WESTERN ROMAN EMPIRE

Rome

Sicily

Carthage

Vandals

BRITAIN
Anglo-Saxons

Bordeaux

SPAIN
Visigoths

NORTH AFRICA

0   100   500
Miles

N

The Late Roman Empire

Glanville Downey
Indiana University

Robert E. Krieger Publishing Company
Malabar, Florida

Original Edition 1969
Reprint 1976

Printed and Published by
ROBERT E. KRIEGER PUBLISHING COMPANY, INC.
KRIEGER DRIVE
MALABAR, FLORIDA 32950

Library of Congress Cataloging-in-Publication Data

Downey, Glanville, 1908-
 The late Roman Empire.

 Reprint of the ed. published by Holt, Rinehart and Winston, New
York in series: Berkshire studies in history.
 Bibliography: p.
 Includes index.
 1. Rome-History-Empire, 284-476.   2. Italy
History-476-1268. I. Title.
[DG311.D65 1977)   937'.06   76-18145
ISBN 0-88275-441-6

10 9 8 7 6 5 4 3

Preface

The purpose of this study is to provide a succinct account of the various factors—political, religious, social, economic, military—that combined to shape the course of history in the Late Roman Empire. It is not a fundamental work and does not undertake to supplant the comprehensive treatments of the period, which are listed in the bibliography. Because of the limit of size appropriate to a study such as the present one, it has often been necessary to select certain material for treatment while other material is passed over. The guiding principle has been twofold, to show the elements that were new in the life of the Late Roman Empire and distinguished it from the empire in its earlier history, and to point out the ideas that developed during this period, especially in the fields of statecraft and religion, that had a permanent effect on the civilization of Europe and the Slavic states.

The chronological limits of the Late Roman Empire are here taken to be the beginning of the reign of Diocletian and the death of Justinian. There are, as is well known, other views as to the definition of the period and the fixing of the chronological point of the beginning of the Byzantine Empire which was the continuation in the East of the Roman Empire. One of the most distinguished historians of the epoch, A. H. M. Jones, begins his account with the accession of Diocletian and closes it with the death of Maurice (A.D. 602). Ernest Stein's *Histoire du Bas-Empire* covers the period A.D. 284–565, while J. B. Bury chose as his limits A.D. 395–565.

In fact the term Late Roman Empire was not used by the writers who lived in that period but is a device adopted by modern scholars, beginning in the eighteenth century, who needed a way of defining the nature of their books. The phrase is, indeed, significant as a recognition that the period has distinctive characteristics which set it off from the earlier period of the history of the Roman Empire. But even though it is necessary in modern times to speak of the Late Roman Empire, it must be remembered that, as the British historian R. G. Collingwood wrote, "There are in history no beginnings. History books begin and end, but the events they describe do not."

I am deeply conscious of my obligation to many scholars who have worked in this field; the extent of my debt may be measured by the list of books in the bibliography on which I have drawn. Likewise I am grateful to four colleagues who read the manuscript, pointed out opportunities for improvement, and saved me from errors.

Bloomington, Indiana   G. D.
February 1969

Contents

The Late
Roman Empire

1 From the Roman Empire to the "Late" Roman Empire

• *The Components of Imperial Rule*   While the Late Roman Empire—here considered to be the period beginning with the reign of Diocletian and ending with the reign of Justinian—exhibited the special historical phenomena that have led scholars to give it a distinctive name, there are certain threads, elements of continuity, that can be traced throughout the history of Roman rule.

One of the oldest, most important threads was the tradition of the eternity and sacred character of the Roman state. As early as in the reign of Augustus, in the last years of the first century B.C., the phrases *Roma aeterna, Urbs aeterna, Urbs sacra*—Eternal Rome, the Eternal City, the Sacred City—appear in the writings of poets and historians. Rome had been founded under divine auspices and had grown to greatness by the favor of the gods of Rome and the virtues of the Roman people. The gods were eternal and so the state and people whom they fostered must be eternal also; and since *Roma* was a city approved and protected by the gods, it was a sacred city. In the time of Augustus, Livy wrote of the rise of Rome to the greatness destined for it by the gods. So long as Rome enjoyed the favor of its divine protectors and conducted its affairs properly, an end to the Roman state was not conceivable. There was no other power in the world like Rome.

Joined with the tradition of the eternity of the state was the tradition of the imperial office as both the instrument and the embodiment of the state. The growth in power and territory of the Roman Republic had brought into being what was in effect a Republican Empire, but the machinery of the old Roman city-state was unable to administer the new territories properly. Augustus created an imperial administration that met the needs of the new world-state. His system, which was in name a continuation and adaptation of the machinery of the republican form of government, was in fact the government of a *princeps*, a "first citizen," ruling on the basis of his personal authority and prestige, and with the consent—even the desire—of the people. Augustus, the first *princeps*, was in many ways the greatest. In part he owed his success to his personal popularity.

The new regime assured peace and prosperity. The emperor, who gradually became a divine figure, stood as the father of the country, the symbol of Rome's power, and the embodiment of continuity. In principle, the state still consisted of the Senate and the Roman people. The emperor was the head of this state and the symbol of its majesty, and a good emperor was bound to be popular; at the same time, according to traditional formality, he needed recognition by the Senate, which by vote confirmed the powers of each emperor in succession. Because he possessed supreme authority, the emperor was also charged with ultimate responsibility. Treason was a crime against the majesty of the Roman people, as incorporated in the emperor. If the imperial rule of necessity had come to be absolute, it also was limited by the recognition that the rule existed in answer to a need, and this entailed a "good" emperor's acceptance of his responsibility.

A further essential aspect of the structure of Roman rule at the time of the origin of the Late Empire was the concept that Roman rule was not only eternal and imperial but universal. The imperial regime was a reflection of Rome's acknowledged destiny, expressed by Vergil, Livy, and Horace, to bring peace and order to the non-Roman peoples. Roman rule assured the security and stable government that guaranteed civilized life for the nations Rome had conquered. Perforce the empire had come to comprise varied peoples, races, and tongues other than Roman and Latin; but it was the essence of the empire that all these peoples were united in one state under a sovereign who was the ruler of such a world because he ruled under divine protection, as a respreseative of divine power, and was himself regarded as being in some sense divine. The ideological concept of the empire was enforced by the Roman legions in the provinces.

A further thread was the joining of two worlds, Greek and Roman. The political structure of the empire was Roman, and the special Roman genius for administration, organization, and law was one of the greatest strengths of the empire. The Latin language reflected all these qualities. But part of Rome's task had been the conquest of the Greek world. This had two consequences. Greece gave a new intellectual and artistic aspect of life to Rome: at the same time Rome provided the Greek world with the secure physical protection and government that enabled Greek culture to survive on its own soil and on its own terms. The aristocrats in the conquered cities welcomed and cooperated with Roman rule; but the Greek cities, allowed by Rome to retain a measure of independence and maintaining their ancient civilization which was their distinctive possession, continued to live in the tradition of their own histories, within, but at the same time independent of, the larger history of the Roman Empire. The survival of the Greek tradition in the eastern half of the empire supplied one of the resources out of which the Late Roman Empire was able to build its new society and culture.

Thus the record of Rome's achievement produced a history such as—the Romans believed—no other nation of the world possessed. The history of the Eternal City and its people constituted visible proof that Rome was destined to be a great power in the civilized world. The Roman historians had a splendid theme—the success of men who were courageous, serious, hard working, prudent, thrifty, obedient to established authority, devoted to the gods, family, home, and country, careful to preserve the demonstrated values of the customs of their ancestors, and slow to adopt a change until it was proved sound. In the old Roman tradition the true Roman put the welfare of the state above his own.

Such was the ancient tradition in the days of the early empire. In the third century A.D. much happened to overshadow both the ideas and their outward expression.

• *The Military Anarchy of the Third Century and the Problem of the Imperial Office* One of the distinctive marks of the Late Roman Empire is that it followed a long crisis during which the state almost disappeared. The crisis had been a time of danger such as Rome had not known since the civil wars of the first century B.C. "The Military Anarchy," as modern scholars have called the fifty years of the middle of the third century, A.D. 235–284, witnessed a tumultuous succession of emperors. In these fifty years there were twenty-four Roman emperors who could be considered to have achieved official recognition; there were assorted pretenders and usurpers in addition. The longest reigns were the seven years of Valerian (253–260) and the eight years of his son Gallienus (260–268). Many of the emperors came to the throne by the assassination of the previous incumbent. Between the death of Severus Alexander (235) and the accession of Diocletian (284), all the emperors save two died violent deaths. The exceptions were Claudius, who died of the plague after a reign of two years, and Valerian, who was taken prisoner by the Persians and died in captivity. One emperor, Decius, reigned for three years and was killed fighting the Goths. The rest were assassinated or killed by rivals in civil wars. It is understandable that a later writer, when compiling a collection of biographies of the emperors or would-be emperors of the period, included a chapter entitled "The Thirty Pretenders."

What lay behind this disorder, unparalleled in the history of Rome? The empire had been powerful. Its long frontiers stretched from Britain along the Rhine and the Danube to the eastern borders of the mountains of Armenia and the desert east of Syria and Palestine. To maintain the security of this empire in peaceful times was a sufficiently demanding task; when any major external threat appeared, the resources of the whole state were taxed.

So it was in the third century, when the barbarians began to press on the northern boundaries and a new regime in Persia, the Sassanids, confronted the Roman government with a new weight of power along a frontier that had always been difficult to defend. The empire's resources could not match the demands that were made upon it. One aspect of the problem was the vast length of the frontiers; the other was the violence of the attacks of the barbarians who were driven by the pressures of growing populations and lack of food, and by the urge to enjoy the material benefits of Roman life which they knew about through the goods they saw in the Roman export trade.

The nature of the emergency had not been foreseen; indeed, in the Roman world of that time it probably could not have been foreseen or provided for. There had come into existence, in the third century, a whole complex of problems that became critical under stress. Some of them had long-standing roots, each had its own origin, but all of them were interconnected. When simultaneous defense of long frontiers was needed, the army proved inadequate. Actually, the economy could not support sufficiently large armies. Agricultural methods, never highly developed, did not produce surpluses of foods, and famines due to weather or crop failure were frequent. The small farmers, always living on a slender margin, often lost their land to the great landowners who had capital, and farm families, an important source of recruits for the army, grew smaller.

At the same time industry was unable to expand production because nothing was done to improve techniques, and slave labor was becoming scarce. Taxes and requisitions to support the cost of foreign and civil wars imposed a heavy strain, especially on the lower and middle classes. The Romans of that day did not understand the real workings of finance and on occasion, when there were extraordinary expenses or periods of high prices, the government resorted to inflation to meet its expenses.

When a number of such problems presented themselves simultaneously, the resources of the government were not always able to deal with them adequately, and it might not always be clear that the critical situation that demanded attention was a symptom and not a cause. For example, agriculture, the principal industry of the empire and the source of most of the national income, suffered badly in the civil wars and barbarian invasions as land was devastated and cattle were requisitioned or carried off. Farmers abandoned their lands. The government's problems in other areas were so pressing that even if it had wished to do so it would have been unable to institute a successful program for the rehabilitation of agriculture.

The financial problems of the municipalities illustrate the difficulty at that time of dealing with fundamental social and economic ills. Traditionally the local landowners and merchants who served as magistrates and formed the local senates in their municipalities had paid for the cost of public buildings and public services as a patriotic duty. When increasing government expenses made higher taxes necessary, the taxes levied on the municipalities were simply increased though there was no way of increasing production and income, and the local aristocracies found their fortunes and their status diminishing.

Here in fact is one example of a general dislocation of the social order in the third century. While peasants were deserting the land, the local leading families were losing in numbers and influence. Many members of the senatorial families of Rome were killed as political enemies when new emperors came to the throne, or became paupers when their property was confiscated. The successive emperors then filled out the Senate by appointing men of lesser rank, often from the provinces. In such conditions, loyalty to the Roman state suffered and the ancient tradition of civic patriotism began to fail.

The growing burdens on all classes of society would have constituted a sufficiently difficult problem under a government that was stable and able to cope with difficulties firmly. But now the state suffered from an additional problem as old as the imperial office itself, namely, the problem of succession. If an able emperor were blessed with an able son, or if he could adopt a worthy colleague, all was well; but an orderly succession did not always occur. The son succeeding a capable father might prove to be unsuitable, or an unworthy family might gain control of the throne for a time. Moreover the Roman army discovered early what Tacitus had called the secret of the empire—an emperor might be created elsewhere than in Rome. When the right moment came, a popular general in one of the provinces might be acclaimed as emperor by his troops, who understood very well the benefits that would come to them if they succeeded in putting their commander in power.

By the time the state had fallen into anarchy, in the third century, the Roman Senate was virtually obsolete, and served chiefly as the visible embodiment of the aristocracy. In the days of the republic the Senate had been the administrative branch of the government and the consuls the executive; but with the development of the monarchy, the civil service bureaus, which functioned directly under the emperor, supplanted the functions of the Senate, and indeed performed them more efficiently. Thus the executive (the monarch) and the administration (the imperial civil service) were fused. The citizenry could no longer serve as the ultimate source of power; the army could not fill this role in responsible fashion. Sometimes the senators could manage to assert some authority in opposition to a weak emperor; but against the power of an army marching on Rome the Senate had no effective weapon, and an emperor who had come into power by force could determine what the status of the Senate in his regime was to be.

When armies and generals saw the terms on which an emperor could be created, the imperial office became a prize and the Senate and people had to accept what the changes of fortune brought them. The imperial career was a hazardous one, for there was seldom a period during the third-century anarchy when the emperor did not have to deal with foreign enemies or rivals at home, sometimes both at once.

All these factors of weakness interacted in such a way that the remedy of one problem could scarcely have relieved the others. The series of soldier-emperors came and went, engaged in wars along the Danube or on the Persian front. When the year of the celebration of the thousandth anniversary of the traditional date of the founding of Rome arrived (247), the emperor was Philip, surnamed The Arabian, an epithet that would scarcely have been thinkable at an earlier period of Roman history. A few years later the Roman people endured a disgrace such as they had never suffered. The emperor Valerian was captured by the Persians and died a prisoner. There were many stories of the humiliations to which he was subjected by the Persians.

Ten years later the first sign of a change in Rome's fortunes appeared when a general came into power who soon proved to be one of the ablest of the Roman sovereigns. Aurelian (270–275), born of a humble family in Illyricum, rose in the army through his notable talents and was placed on the throne by the army at the age of fifty-five. The first problem with which he dealt was the restoration of discipline in the army; the troops, knowing that it was possible for them to make or unmake an emperor, had become arrogant and slack.

In a series of rapid campaigns Aurelian defeated the barbarians in Pannonia and on the Danube and put an end to rebellions in Gaul and Palmyra. At the same time he accomplished badly needed reforms. He restored the coinage, which had become debased. The services of bakers and shippers, so necessary to the economy, were given both support and control by placing their guilds under official supervision. This device of controlling workers in essential occupations was to be more and more widely employed until in the early part of the fourth century the government exercised a close control over most kinds of production.

During the years of anarchy the transitory emperors had enjoyed little of the personal prestige of the earlier sovereigns of more orderly times, and the traditional official cult of the ruler, along with the worship of the goddess Roma, could hardly possess its earlier significance. Aurelian added to the ideological apparatus of the imperial office the worship of the sun god. Long familiar in Syria, and well-known to the army units that had served there, this cult served to lend a new aura of divinity to the emperor's person, when it was announced that the sun—now called "Lord Sun"—was the "companion," helper and guardian of the emperor.

The emperor's notable gifts as commander and administrator were cut off when he was murdered by some of his own officers. Another Illyrian soldier-emperor, Probus (276–282), had a few years in which to continue Aurelian's program and preserve peace on the frontiers, but he too was murdered by mutinous troops in return for his efforts to maintain tight discipline.

• *Diocletian and the Reconstruction of the State* Though Aurelian and Probus were not permitted to accomplish all that they might have, the work of reconstruction was taken up by Diocletian (284–305), one of the most remarkable personalities among all the Roman emperors. He, also an Illyrian of modest origin, possessed talents that brought him to the top in the army; only this time it was a different kind of talent.

One of Diocletian's advantages was that he came into power, at the age of about fifty-nine, only after years of observing the state's problems. His observation had been intelligent, and when he found the opportunity, Diocletian left his mark on every department of the government.

Increased efficiency was gained by separating military and civil command in the provinces and in the upper levels of the government. The army was enlarged and more efficiently organized, and state-owned factories for the manufacture of weapons and uniforms were established. The central administration was overhauled, and to reduce administrative burdens, the provinces were divided and reduced in size, and grouped in administrative units called dioceses. Another purpose of the reduction was to obviate the danger of rebellion by a governor of a large and powerful province such as Syria.

The changes in the army and the civil service were significant not only for the efficiency of the government but for the whole social structure of the empire. Increased in size and in privileges, the army and the civil service began to constitute an elite caste which was in effect self-perpetuating. Economically, these branches of the government added to the problems of the day because they were not only non-productive themselves but they required more and more of the services and the products of the agricultural and industrial elements, as well as an increasing share of the government's income in taxes and requisitions.

A reform of the first importance was the institution of a new system of taxation of land, animals, and the agricultural population. The productive land in the empire was inventoried and classified so that it could be assessed for taxation purposes in terms of the nature of its products and its fertility. The labor of the men and animals was assessed for taxation in the same way. It was now possible to forecast with fair accuracy what the income of the state would be from these sources.

To assure production, peasants were compelled by law to

remain on the ground they were cultivating, and a beginning was made of the process, later extended, of compelling workers in other areas of production to remain in their occupations. In the municipalities, the sons of the local landowners who constituted the local senates were henceforth required to follow their fathers and assume their financial obligations.

Reform of the debased coinage was one of the most pressing of Diocletian's problems. For a century or more, inflation had reduced the value of the currency to the point that people no longer had confidence in the coins and business suffered seriously. The solution Diocletian attempted, the institution of a uniform imperial coinage to replace the independent issues the local mints had been putting out, was a logical step but it proved impossible to carry the reform to completion. In 301 the emperor issued an Edict of Maximum Prices, the real purpose of which cannot now be determined. The edict may have represented an effort to stop the rise of prices that the coinage reform had been unable to arrest, or it may have been meant only to serve as an interim control during the period when the old worthless currency was being replaced by the new. In any case, price control proved impossible to enforce. Goods were withdrawn from sale, and the controls had to be given up.

Recent experience had shown that the empire in a time of crisis needed some form of imperial administration which was better prepared for prompt and effective military action than the traditional pattern of the sole Augustus, with or without a colleague or a junior designated as his successor. Diocletian devised a new plan, partly based on existing precedents. There was precedent for an emperor to appoint a fully qualified colleague with the title of Augustus (Marcus Aurelius, 161–180, and Lucius Verus, 161–169), and also precedent for an emperor to adopt a successor and to give him the title of Caesar (Hadrian, 117–138, and L. Aelius, 136–138). Diocletian elaborated these precedents into a new scheme of government called the Tetrarchy, or "rule of four." The eastern and western halves of the empire were to be divided between two Augusti; one was to be senior but each was to have full imperial powers. To each Augustus there would be attached a younger colleague, with the title Caesar, who would be trained to succeed his Augustus when the latter died or retired. Each new Augustus would then appoint a Caesar.

The plan had the merit, in principle, of distributing the burdens of rule and of forestalling the chaos that might follow the sudden death of a sole emperor. In practice the arrangement proved unworkable; but in its recognition of the need for a regular provision for the simultaneous presence of competent rulers in both the eastern and western divisions of the empire, Diocletian's scheme had an important influence on the future of both the imperial administration and the military establishment. The difficulty of maintaining a harmonious collegiality of rulers in East and West, with equal authority and equal resources of strength, was one of the factors that led to the ultimate division of the two halves of the empire into separate parts which enjoyed different fortunes; the Roman power in the West declined and was replaced by the barbarian kingdoms, while the eastern empire maintained its independence and developed into the Byzantine state. Thus, although Diocletian's Tetrarchy failed to be a permanent form of administration, it was portentous of the future.

A corollary of the division of East and West between two Augusti was the need for a new capital in the East. Rome as the capital of the West was no longer an efficient center for the administration of the whole empire. Diocletian established a new capital for the eastern division at Nicomedia (which was eventually replaced, under Constantine the Great, by Constantinople). At the same time Diocletian organized a mobile court which could accompany him on his inspection trips and military campaigns.

One of the most serious needs that Diocletian perceived was the re-establishment of the prestige and authority of the

Diocletian. Portrait found at Nicomedia, now in the Archaeological Museum, Istanbul. (*Hirmer Verlag, Munich*)

emperor, which had been badly shaken during the military anarchy. Diocletian's reign marks the final passage from the Principate, which could claim to have grown out of republican ideals, to the autocratic regime of a ruler with absolute power. Here as elsewhere Diocletian stressed continuity with earlier Roman traditions; at the same time the monarchy was transformed in an essential way. The emperor now rarely appeared in public and when he did make himself visible, his appearance occasioned a public festival. The increasing remoteness of the emperor was emphasized by his elaborate insignia; with the state increasingly militarized, military uniform became the emperor's customary dress.

It was not only in outward appearance that Diocletian sought to heighten the majesty of the imperial office; the spiritual sanction as well had to be strengthened. In both republic and empire, public religion had always been a department of the government, and it had been one of the strongest Roman traditions that the prosperity and success of Rome had depended not only on the Roman people but on the gods of Rome. The public cult of the goddess Roma and of the emperors who had been deified after death had served as an effective symbol of unity and on occasion as a test of political loyalty; but public respect for this imperial worship had suffered during the anarchy.

Aurelian had sought to put the worship of the emperor on a new footing by introducing the cult of the sun and by declaring himself to be under the protection of this god. Now Diocletian, always conservative and always seeking to maintain and strengthen the ancient idea of Rome, proclaimed a doctrine that again placed the imperial office under the protection of the ancient Roman gods, but in new terms. The senior Augustus in the East, and his junior colleague Maximian, Augustus of the West, were proclaimed to be under the protection of two of the most powerful Roman divinities. Jupiter, representing wisdom and rule, was announced to be the "companion" and "preserver" of Diocletian, and Hercules, representing strength, obedience, and service, performed a similar role for Maximian. The Augusti were now supposed to be the earthly representatives of these gods; the spirits of the gods were supposed to be actually at work in their imperial protégés. The imperial office thus gained added prestige and influence which later carried over into the reigns of the Christian emperors.

The court ceremonial reflected this divine aura. Persons who approached the emperor were required to prostrate themselves in the act of *proskynesis*, the traditional oriental posture of the adoration of divine majesty. *Dominus*, "Lord," became the customary form of address to the emperor. The Principate became the Dominate.

While Diocletian's conservative policy emphasized traditional official worship, the growth of the Christian community had brought it to the point at which it could constitute a real political problem. Though not numerous, Christians were conspicuous because their belief forbade them to perform the ritual acts of the state religion. Moreover, some prominent persons were known to be interested in the cult. Christians made it plain that they regarded themselves as different from, and better than, pagans, and put themselves in the position of refusing to perform the profession of loyalty to the state. From time to time (most recently under Valerian, in 257) the government had persecuted and punished disloyal subjects. Punishment included deportation, hard labor in government mines and quarries, torture, maiming, and often death. However, these persecutions, which sometimes were of a local character, had failed to halt the spread of the cult, and there had not been a systematic enforcement of the regulations dealing with Christians since the end of Valerian's reign. The Christian community continued to grow.

Diocletian during the early part of his reign maintained the tacit toleration of the Christians that had been in effect since 260. However, there were fanatical enemies of the

Christians among the high officials around Diocletian, the most conspicuous being Galerius, Diocletian's Caesar. Persecution of peculiar people who were conspicuous as un-Roman and subversive could be a useful program for an ambitious politician. Alarm was raised when it was discovered that there were Christian soldiers and officers among the troops on duty at the imperial palace itself. Diocletian dealt with the danger by expelling Christians from the army and by compelling some to leave the court.

When the twentieth anniversary of Diocletian's reign (November, 303) approached, and his age, in the seventies, made it plain that he could not expect to direct affairs for many more years, the forces hostile to the Christians launched a major attack. An incident at Nicomedia provided the occasion. Christian troops at an official religious ceremony were seen to cross themselves. To a Christian, this act would ward off the powers of pagan demons; but to the pagan authorities, the gesture would amount to a kind of magical spell which would anger the pagan gods and invalidate the ritual of the ceremony. Enemies of the Christians could say that such an act subverted the discipline of the army and undermined the authority of the state.

Diocletian was persuaded that there was serious danger, and an edict was posted on February 23, 303, inaugurating one of the severest persecutions in the experience of the Church. The intention was to force Christians to return to the official worship of the pagan gods of the state. If they refused, they lost their privileges as Roman citizens. All churches were to be closed and all copies of the Christian scriptures were to be given up to be burned. All Christians were deprived of any official honors and offices that they held.

When two fires in succession broke out in the palace, the Christians were blamed, and a second edict ordered the arrest of all Christian clergy. The church in Nicomedia was pillaged and demolished by troops. The clergy were to be forced either to recant or to be imprisoned and tortured, and possibly executed. Finally, in 304, the necessity of recantation was made applicable to all Christians, with the same penalties. This was the beginning of the last empire-wide persecution of the Christians.

Such was the position of the problem of the Christians when Diocletian, at the age of nearly eighty, abdicated on May 1, 305. Under his successors, the changes in the Tetrarchy put the problem on a different footing, politically.

One of the writers of the following generation called Diocletian "the man whom the state needed." In view of what the recent history of Rome had been, it was a remarkable enough feat for an emperor to have remained on the throne for twenty-one years and then to have abdicated voluntarily; this was a longer reign, indeed, than any since that of Antoninus Pius (138–161). But even so the new direction of the history of Rome was not yet wholly visible. It remained for Constantine the Great to complete the rebuilding of the state—and in a direction that Diocletian would not have anticipated.

2 The First
Christian Emperor

• *Constantine and East Rome* Like many early saints of
the church, St. Constantine, emperor of the Romans, was
born a pagan. The process by which Flavius Valerius Constantinus became the Imperator Caesar Constantinus
Augustus, *pontifex maximus*, Father of the Fatherland, the
thirteenth apostle, and was canonized, is the central theme
of the remarkable history of the Roman people between the
years 306 and 337.

Constantine (born *ca.* 280, died 337) had the advantage
of being the son of Constantius Chlorus, who had been
appointed Caesar in the West by Diocletian in 293 and
later advanced to the rank of Augustus of the West. Constantine while still a boy was sent to the court of Diocletian.
This apprenticeship gave him an opportunity to observe
the tasks of a Tetrarch and the workings of the machinery
of the state. Although Diocletian's program had saved the
empire from the worst dangers of the military anarchy, the
Roman world was still far from peaceful. There were revolts successively in Britain, Egypt, and Africa. Constantine
was a companion of Diocletian when the emperor was
summoned to Egypt (296–297) to deal with the disorders
there.

The events that shaped Constantine's career began while
he was still young. When Diocletian and his colleague Maximian abdicated (305) in favor of their Caesars, Constantius Chlorus and Galerius became Augusti of West and

East respectively, with Severus and Maximinus Daia as their Caesars.

Outwardly the change took place according to plan, and for the time being the efficient continuation of the Tetrarchy seemed assured. However, it became evident that, deprived of the firm control of Diocletian, the theory of the Tetrarchy could not be maintained in the face of the personal ambitions of the junior members and of army officers who found themselves in command of enough military force to attempt to seize power for themselves.

Among these struggles for power Constantine's own advance began. When his father became Augustus, Constantine left the eastern court and joined him, and when Constantius died (306) the troops proclaimed their general's son Augustus. Like the youthful Octavian at the death of Julius Caesar, three and a half centuries before, Constantine was put in a position of danger and opportunity as a very young man; his training had prepared him for the struggle that lay ahead. In the next years the new Augusti and their Caesars had to defend themselves against the attacks of adventurous generals attempting to seize power. In one year (307) there were four men who claimed to be Augusti, including Constantine.

With rule divided among different members of a Tetrarchy, and with would-be rulers contending for power, persecution of Christians began to take on a new political aspect. The edicts of persecution began to be enforced in different parts of the empire with varying degrees of strictness, depending on the personal religious views and the political aspirations of the Augusti and Caesars; and the structure of the Tetrarchy made it possible for a change to take place in the tempo of persecution whenever a new member took office. In the West, Constantius, as Caesar, had not gone beyond closing the churches, and there seem to have been no martyrdoms in Britain and Gaul.

Constantine had observed the official attempts to deal with the problem of the Christians, and the constancy of these people to their religious ideas impressed him, as it did other pagan officials. When Diocletian's program of the reconstruction of the state was still going forward, any element of disloyalty among the citizens was dangerous, and Roman law had always prescribed some of the most painful penalties for treason. Intelligent officials had observed that in the face of these terrible threats some Christians were willing to renounce their subversive religion and make the required profession of loyalty. But there were many who could not be induced by the most severe torture or the threat of the most painful death to change. These people's spectacular constancy actually made converts to their religion. In the eastern half of the empire, the domain of the fiercely anti-Christian Galerius, persecution had been most intense. Here the presence of a body of obstinate Christians, attracting popular attention, constituted a political factor in the plans of both Galerius and his rivals.

Early in 311 there was in fact a remarkable change in the persecution. Galerius had contracted a painful disease, which he believed was the vengeance of the god of the Christians. On April 30 he issued an edict of toleration which accorded legal recognition to Christians. They now had the right to individual freedom of conscience and the right to assemble for worship, so long as they did "nothing contrary to good order." Galerius died painfully a few days after the publication of the decree, and the Christians greeted his suffering and death as a sign of the power of God.

It was in the following year, according to a tradition which was unclear in antiquity and has been a subject for debate among modern scholars, that the Christian deity was supposed to have actually intervened in the affairs of Constantine. In his official capacity, Constantine had had Apollo as his divine companion and protector. According to the tradition, however, in 312, at a critical point in his struggle for power, Constantine actually turned to Christianity, reportedly as a result of a direct communication from the deity. In a traditional Roman empire, this was surely one of the most surprising things that an emperor could do.

Constantine's act—one of the most celebrated conversions in the history of the Church—was a turning point in the history of Europe. The consequences, in the establishment of the Christian Roman Empire and the tradition of Christian monarchy, are evident; but the surviving ancient records of Constantine's own experience are sparse and enigmatic. It has been impossible to determine the emperor's motives and the real nature of his conversion, in the religious sense. Much of the evidence reflects the sudden joy of the triumphant Church. However, the circumstances of the time make it seem possible that Constantine's action was a political expedient, designed to gain the support of the Christians. It is also possible to believe on the basis of Constantine's later history that the conversion was the result of a real religious experience.

An account of the episode has been preserved which is supposed to have been written by Constantine's friend and adviser, Eusebius, the scholarly bishop of Caesarea in Palestine, to whom Constantine, many years later, was supposed to have related his experience. The account presents difficulties and its authorship by Eusebius has been questioned, but whether it is an official account or a legend, it has become famous.

In 312, the contest for power had reached a point at which there had to be an encounter between Constantine and his rival Maxentius, who held the city of Rome. This might be a decisive battle. Constantine, in Gaul, set out with his army for Rome. According to the tradition, as the crisis approached Constantine began to understand that events had shown that the pagan gods had failed to support their worshipers in the struggle for power. Constantine knew of the Christian god, and knew that his father had been sufficiently interested in this god to be lenient to the Christians. This thought brought hope, and Constantine prayed to his father's god. The supernatural help was ready and Constantine was granted a vision, at noon, as the army was on the march. The vision—stated to have been seen by the soldiers as well as by Constantine—was a cross of light in the sky, above the sun, accompanied by an inscription, BY THIS CONQUER. While Constantine was still pondering the meaning of this sign, Christ appeared to him in a dream and instructed him to place on the shields of his soldiers the monogram *chi rho*, ☧, the initial letters of the name of Christ in Greek, and in this way to go into battle. Constantine obeyed and defeated Maxentius in the battle of the Milvian Bridge outside Rome (October, 312). Maxentius was killed in the battle and Constantine was proclaimed Augustus by the Senate. The Milvian Bridge was a spectacular victory, won against heavy odds, and it put Constantine far along in his climb to power.

Constantine joined forces with Licinius, the heir of Galerius, who was seeking to make himself master of the East. Each issued an edict of toleration (Constantine in 312, Licinius in 313) which granted complete freedom to Christianity as well as to all other religions. Confiscated property was restored to the churches.

A final phase in Constantine's career began. Relations with Licinius proved unstable because of rival interests. After two wars between them, Constantine won a decisive battle at Chrysopolis on the Bosporus (324). Licinius, forced to abdicate, later was executed. For the first time in many years the empire was effectively united under a single emperor.

One of his first acts was the foundation of his new capital Constantinople, "Constantine's City," on the site of the old Greek City of Byzantium. Strategically the location was excellent; and Constantine gained prestige from founding a new capital rather than occupying an existing one.

• *Emperor and People* Constantine's personal history and his rise to power illustrate the character the imperial office had come to have in the Late Roman Empire. The position of the emperor in this period, and the nature of the society

Constantine the Great. Head of a statue from the Basilica of Maxentius, now in the Palazzo dei Conservatori, Rome. (*Hirmer Verlag, Munich*)

over which he ruled, will help to explain some of the difficulties of the Roman state at this epoch.

The emperor was an individual filling an office that had existed before him and would, it was taken for granted, continue to exist after him. The office was identical with the empire and so was perpetual; the historian Tacitus, writing in the early years of the second century, had represented the emperor Tiberius as saying that princes were mortal, but the state was eternal. The emperor's office also was sacred and gave sanctity to the person of the emperor. Before the time of Constantine, official deification after death and divine honors during life expressed the gratitude of the people for the more than human qualities that alone could enable the emperor to rule successfully so great an empire. The emperor Domitian (81-96) had unsuccessfully demanded that he be addressed as "Lord and God"; but these epithets became a regular part of the titles of Aurelian and Diocletian.

With sanctity went power, both theoretical and actual. The history of the imperial office had been one of a continual extension of the emperor's activities into new administrative areas, bringing a steady accretion of new functions and powers that in succeeding reigns came to be established as customary. It was inevitable that the Roman emperor should come to possess what amounted to unlimited authority.

The parallel growth of the civil service provided the instrument for the exercise of centralized and autocratic rule. The civil service had originated under Augustus as a part of the imperial household. At first the civil servants were a professional clerical staff appointed personally by the emperor to assist him in his own particular administrative duties as distinguished from the duties that still at that time fell to the Senate. As the power of the emperor increased, the civil service grew until it constituted the essential administrative machinery of the government. In the Late Roman Empire the official character of the service was emphasized by its being organized on military lines, and its members wore a species of uniform bearing insignia of rank.

At the same time, the members of the civil service continued to be regarded in their original character as members of the imperial household. In the Late Roman Empire each member of the bureaucracy, from the highest cabinet officer to the most humble clerk keeping tax records in a village, was regarded as a personal representative of the emperor, possessing an extension of his power and bearing a part of his authority. This concept was reinforced by the presence, in civil service offices throughout the empire, of official portraits of the emperor sent from Constantinople. These were considered embodiments of the sovereign. They possessed the sanctity that attached to his person; violence offered to an imperial portrait amounted to treason.

The civil service was inevitably subject to the abuses possible in a bureaucracy. It tended to become larger and larger, more and more complex, and more and more devoted to the preservation of official forms. The paper work was enormous. Too often the functionaries took advantage of their position to oppress the citizens. But in that time and place the civil service was as efficient as could be expected and the chiefs of divisions and other responsible heads often were men of outstanding ability.

As an instrument of the imperial office, the civil service played an essential role in preserving the stability of the empire, assuring the continuity of the work of the government in spite of any violent change that might take place in the occupancy of the imperial office itself. When there was violent change, the heads of the divisions might be replaced but the lower functionaries would continue at work. The imperial office and the civil service together formed a kind of monolithic organism. At the same time the civil service, as an indispensable self-contained and self-perpetuating entity, gave essential support to the continuous existence of the imperial office as a permanent institution.

Although the imperial office was permanent and gave its incumbent vast powers, the emperors found that their conduct was subject to limitation in a number of ways. The emperor in office was an official figure, a symbol of the government, and at the same time an individual who had at one time in his life not been emperor, perhaps not even a member of a ruling house. Before coming to office he might have been only one of several possible candidates. When he became emperor, if he did not eliminate these other individuals, they might become his rivals or antagonists.

Even if there were no danger from rivals, the emperor had to reckon with the social classes and special interest groups of which his empire was composed. These groups were capable of mustering considerable power. It was always possible for an emperor to be overthrown, and on occasion a pretender could call upon substantial support from dissatisfied subjects.

The most conspicuous of such groups, certainly the one the most capable of decisive action, was the army, including the palace guard. The senior officers, especially those who through ability or intrigue had succeeded in obtaining appointments at court, were either the most immediate source of support or the most immediate threat to the emperor. A commander in the capital was in an excellent position when the throne became vacant. The soldiers themselves knew that they could improve their position by putting forward a popular general as a candidate; they could also look for competitive bids for support from rival candidates.

Another unit which possessed influence of a different, and in some ways more extensive, kind, was the aristocracy. Like the imperial office, the aristocracy represented one of the continuing traditions of Roman society, in which a distinct gulf between the upper class and the common people had always been accepted as the normal structure of society. Controlling land and wealth, and maintaining and extending its influence through arranged marriages and through patronage in the civil service, the law, and the army, the aristocracy could furnish either effective support or effective opposition to an emperor. In the case of emperors whose personal origin was not noble, it might prove expedient for the interests of the aristocracy to form an alliance with the ruling house. In the other direction, when an emperor's policies ran counter to the interests of the aristocracy, it was easy for the leading nobles to put forward a contender for the throne who possessed a prestigious name and important financial backing.

A further political element, whose power was often unpredictable but could be very great, was the common people. The Romans of the Late Roman Empire were subjects, rather than citizens, but they still constituted a political force. When a new emperor was elected, formality still required that the acclamation of the people of the capital be added to those of the Senate and the army.

Under both the republic and the empire the basic characteristics of the common people in the capitals, Rome and later Constantinople, remained the same. Both the faulty economic structure and the political system created a city mob that was chronically unemployed and in fact in large part unemployable. The government sporadically attempted to deal with unemployment by providing public works, but the typical device was to provide "bread and entertainments." Expecting its dole and its free shows, the city mob lived in an idleness that was potentially dangerous because of the high rate of illiteracy, or semiliteracy, which was an invitation to demagogues. Degrading slum conditions had their emotional effect. Many of the working people who did not exist on the dole lived on the edge of starvation, and slaves of the great houses were better off. But, in a society based on an authoritarian conception of the nature of government, and on a tradition of wide economic, social, and educational differences between the upper classes and the common people, the existence of the city mob seemed natural. Generations of emperors tolerated their existence without being able to do away with the basic causes of the evil.

In the Late Empire the political potential of the common

people of the great cities showed itself in an organized form that had to be recognized by the government, namely the rival parties of the public chariot races. In the earlier days of the empire the chariot races provided by the authorities, as one of the most popular forms of public entertainment, constituted an outlet for popular enthusiasm centering about favorite stables and drivers. When in action, the charioteers wore identifying colors of red, white, green, and blue.

In the Late Empire the two principal factions, the Blues and the Greens, as they were called, became rallying points for social, political, and theological passions. These parties provided an outlet for complaints against the government's policies, or against the conduct of individual officials, that the government had to regard as salutary, as a kind of safety-valve, and the factions were officially recognized to the extent that the emperors were expected to declare their personal adherence to one or the other. At the same time, of course, there always existed the possibility that the mobs might get out of hand; rioting and bloodshed were not infrequent. The government attempted to maintain a monopoly of the manufacture of weapons, but the mobs always seemed to be able to get hold of arms when they wanted them.

Beginning with the time of Diocletian and Constantine the chariot races had been public occasions on which the emperor and his people met officially. The emperor in his loge, surrounded by dignitaries, received the acclamations of the people; in the time of Justinian, at least, it was permissible for them to present their grievances through a herald who addressed the emperor. This occasion for the official relationship of emperor and people was symbolized by the fact that in the great eastern cities in which there were imperial residences in the Late Empire—Constantinople, Thessalonica, and Antioch—the hippodrome was adjacent to the palace, just as the Circus Maximus at Rome lay just below the imperial residence on the Palatine.

Thus the emperor, ruling without a written constitution, depended on a tradition, a body of precedent, and an accumulation of administrative powers, while his tenure depended on a number of sources of support or opposition which he must know how to manage. There had been revolutions in the history of the Roman Empire but they had been directed against occupants of the imperial office and had never aimed at the return of the republic.

• *The Christian Emperor and the Christian State* Conversion of the emperor to Christianity posed a constitutional problem of a kind that the empire had not previously faced. There was no written constitution with a proviso as to the personal religion of the sovereign. This would in fact have been unnecessary. From the beginning of Roman history the state had prospered through the favor of the gods of Rome and it was the responsibility of the government to preserve that favor by offering the gods their proper worship. When the republic was transformed into an empire, the emperor as head of the state served as *pontifex maximus*, chief priest of the state religion, and as such was responsible for the good relationship of the state and its people with the gods. Here, as in other aspects of the imperial office, the emperor was in effect a representative of the Roman people. Constantine before his conversion had had Apollo as his protector. How could a Roman emperor, one of whose traditional titles was *pontifex maximus*, with one of the traditional gods of Rome as his special guardian, be one of the community of Christians, who had been under persecution as public enemies?

Neither constitutional theory nor historical tradition provided for such a situation; but the character of the imperial office had become such that it was possible for the emperor to initiate innovation when this could be successsfully effected. Aurelian and Diocletian had already made important changes in the ideology of the emperor's position. In fact, the absence of a written constitution was one of the reasons why the imperial office, being capable of being adapted to new conditions, had survived unforeseen vicissitudes.

Whatever Constantine and his Christian advisers may have hoped for, it was not going to be possible to convert the whole empire to Christianity at once, or even soon. There were prominent persons who followed the emperor's example, whether from prudence or from conviction; but there remained a substantial party at court who attempted to persuade Constantine that the old religion was best, and many leading civil officials and high army officers remained pagans. Constantine's position was not an easy one. The imperial coins continued for some time to bear the familiar pagan inscriptions and the religious symbols of the pagan state cult, and it was only gradually that Christian devices were placed on the coins. Constantine, for a time at least, would have to be emperor to two different kinds of subjects, pagans and Christians.

For the Christians, Constantine as a Christian would be acceptable as head of the state, but for them he would be a different kind of Roman emperor. To the Christians, the world and its people were created and governed by God, and it was within such an order that the Roman emperor had his place. The idea of Christian kingship was familiar from the historical books of the Old Testament, and it was not difficult to formulate a Christian ideology of the office of Roman emperor.

The learned Bishop Eusebius of Caesarea contributed to the celebration of the thirtieth anniversary of Constantine's rule (335) a congratulatory oration in which he described the new official ideology of the imperial office. The earthly realm was a *mimesis*, a counterpart, of the kingdom of heaven, and as God ruled in heaven, the emperor ruled on earth. The emperor was not simply a vice-regent of God with a limited appointment and the limited powers of a vice-regent; he was actually God's vice-gerent, appointed as his special representative and deputy. Chosen for his task by

God, the emperor was guided in his decisions by God through the medium of the Holy Spirit. The emperor, understanding his task and his responsibility, must always look to God in the conduct of his office. If his position as representative of God on earth gave the emperor absolute power, it also gave him complete responsibility, both for his official acts and for the religious well-being of his subjects. As God's representative, it was his duty to eradicate unbelief and doctrinal error and to lead his people to the truth.

The position of the Christian emperor had to be different from that of his pagan predecessors because he was to govern a different kind of society. His subjects were sons of God and brothers of Christ as well as subjects of himself. At the same time the emperor, as a person, was a son of God and brother of Christ, and a Christian brother of his subjects. The pagan emperor had had an official personality. The Christian emperor had a new official personality.

The new theory of the imperial power involved no radical departure. Constantine and his successors continued to keep most of the traditional forms of the imperial office. The Christian emperors down to the time of Valentinian I (364–375) and Gratian (375–383) continued to bear the title *pontifex maximus*. In Constantinople a statue was set up of Constantine wearing a radiate crown and facing the sun; an inscription compared Constantine with the sun.

As the Roman emperor was a living symbol of the Roman state and people, the imperial capital was a symbol of another kind, and, like the office, physically durable. In Constantine's day the new capital on the Bosporus was spoken of as "New Rome," a phrase—not an official title—that indicated that the new capital was heir to the authority of the old Rome. The old public structures of Byzantium had been repaired, and splendid new official buildings and churches were erected, whose magnificence strained the government's financial resources. Constantinople, at its dedication on May 11, 330, was a visible symbol

of the success of Constantine's regime, and its churches,
built by the emperor, were symbols of the new position of
Christianity in the state.

The emperor's achievement of sole power enabled him to
continue the transformation of the Roman social and economic system that had been begun by Diocletian. The army
and the bureaucracy were further enlarged and became
even more prominent as the elite orders of Roman society.
To assure economic production and adequate maintenance
of the machinery of government and defense, closer controls
of commerce and manufacture were instituted. In a society
accustomed by long tradition to respect constituted authority, the regulation of the affairs of the citizens was not a
novelty. The physical requirements of the state were considered paramount.

The government obtained its own requirements by re-
quisitioning food, needed materials, and the services of
artisans and laborers. Taxes and government wages were
still often paid in goods rather than in money. Craftsmen
and shopkeepers increasingly were organized in official
guilds which made it possible for the authorities to control
the collection of taxes and the use of raw materials. Mines
and stone quarries were government monopolies, and certain essential occupations, such as that of baker, continued
to be made hereditary.

An important social change of the age of Constantine was
the emergence of the Christian clergy as a new social class
who, in addition to their religious duties, enjoyed special
economic privileges as well as a position of prestige in a
society which had always paid regard to rank. In order to
enhance the dignity of the clergy, Constantine exempted
them from the performance of public services which were
obligatory on other citizens of the same status in the municipalities. In this way the clergy joined the civil service and
the army as a self-perpetuating and privileged sociological
group. One of the economic consequences of the growth of
the clerical order was that manpower which might have

been devoted to other purposes was given over to the service of the Church. Laws had to be passed to prevent men from seeking ordination in order to escape their public obligations, including military service.

The financial problems of the municipalities continued. Increasingly, public services and municipal finances were brought under the control of officials sent out by the central government. The regulations and the activities of the officials were designed in such a way that the central government was relieved of the actual performance of its local functions, while the machinery of the civil service supervised the public services and ensured their proper performance. The magistrates of the cities, elected from among the local men of property, who were expected to provide public buildings and entertainment and to collect the tribute for the government, found themselves being ruined by their burdens. The whole system of municipal government threatened to break down. When many citizens fled from their cities to escape their obligations, laws were passed compelling them to return to their duties. The local aristocracies and middle class, who should have formed one of the sources of strength of the empire, were discouraged and began to decline both in numbers and in influence. Yet this was the only way, in the world of that day, it was considered possible to maintain the vast, costly structure of the government and to achieve the needed social and economic reform.

The restoration of peace and of hope for the future was commemorated in the mottoes which the government placed on the coins to give publicity to its programs. The themes of security, safety, and hope for the state (SECVRITAS REI PVBLICAE, SALVS REI PVBLICAE, SPES REI PVBLICAE) were joined with reminders of the forethought of the rulers for the state (PROVIDENTIA AVGVSTORVM). The figure of the goddess Victory appeared, and the fame of the army was celebrated (GLORIA EXERCITVS). The ancient symbol of the she-wolf nursing Romulus and Remus served as a reminder of the continuity of the state with its ancient origins. In his titles, Constantine was the direct heir of Augustus. The empire was still the empire of Augustus, adapting itself to new needs.

• *The Church and the Bright New Era*   St. Jerome, who was accustomed to speaking his mind, once wrote that the Church by its emancipation under Constantine had gained in material position and wealth, but had lost its true spiritual life. Changes of many kinds inevitably followed when the Church was suddenly transformed into a public institution. From being an illicit and persecuted cult, it found itself in a position of prestige which brought a sudden increase in membership, new wealth, and political influence. Now that the Church was secure in its ownership of real estate, people gave or bequeathed property, often as a token of thanksgiving, sometimes in hope that such gifts would benefit their souls. Unavoidably the clergy found themselves increasingly preoccupied with such mundane matters.

On a higher level the Church could look to the government for material benefits—church buildings, endowments, privileges for the clergy, political support. There came into being a class of worldly prelates who found it to the advantage of their dioceses, and to their own benefit, to spend their time at the imperial court, where competition for imperial favor might call for worldly talents.

Perils such as these do not seem to have been foreseen by the churchmen of the period before Constantine's reign. The records of the Church councils. under Constantine show that the bishops had to spend time on mundane matters and on new questions such as whether the clergy might be married, or, if already married, must separate from their wives.

But not only mundane matters became acute. There were basic points of belief that had been debated before the time of Constantine but had not been satisfactorily settled. The most important of these problems, which was also going to

prove the most difficult to resolve, was how to formulate a
satisfactory statement of the nature of Christ and his relationship to God the Father and to the Holy Spirit. The
whole doctrine of the Trinity was proving to be one of the
most difficult teachings of the Church to explain to in-
quirers and converts; indeed not all Christians found the
doctrine easy to understand. But within the problem of the
Trinity, the question of the nature of the divinity of Christ
took priority, for this concerned the nature and indeed the
validity of the salvation that the Church offered.

The New Testament depicted a Christ who was both
divine and human, and it was difficult for the unin-
structed to understand how both a divine and a human
nature could have been united in a body that was visibly
physical. The problem was crucial, for redemption and
salvation offered by a truly divine person were quite different from redemption and salvation offered by a person who
was not fully divine, or perhaps indeed had no divine character. If Christ were the Son of God, and were fully divine,
did this mean that there were two Gods? Was the Son as
fully God as the Father? Did this mean that in Christianity,
as in the pagan cults, there was a plurality of gods? On the
other hand, if the Son were less fully divine than the
Father, he would, as a less divine person, be subordinate to
the Father. In this case there would seem to be something
like a hierarchy of gods such as pagans were familiar with
in their pantheon. In fact the notion of a subordinate
Christ, divine but less fully divine than the Father, might
make it easier for some pagans to accept Christianity.

This Christological problem had begun to be a matter of
concern among scholars of the Church in the middle and
latter part of the third century. The problem was important enough to lead to the development of rival systems of
theological thought in the schools at Antioch and Alexandria. In the reign of Constantine the problem became
acute as a consequence of the success of the teaching of
Arius, a priest in Alexandria. Arius asserted that the Son

was in some sense later in existence than the Father because
there must have been a time when the Son did not yet exist,
and that the Father must have created the Son out of nothing because the substance of the Father, by its nature, must
be indivisible.

Arius' teaching seemed logical to many people, and it
spread sufficiently to call for investigation by Arius' superior, the bishop of Alexandria. The teaching was condemned by a council of Egyptian bishops and Arius was
excommunicated. But the doctrine had sufficient appeal to
enable Arius to gain support outside of Egypt, and the
controversy grew until there was a major split in the eastern part of the Church. There was a war of pamphlets. The
laity of all ranks took sides passionately, disputing the theological issues among themselves and supporting their local
bishops in their contests with bishops of opposing views. It
was typical of the major theological controversies of the
Late Empire that they were not confined to internal clerical
struggles within the Church but involved the whole Christian population.

While the Arian controversy was troubling the eastern
provinces, another dispute of a different character had
arisen in North Africa. This concerned the status of Christians who in the recent persecutions had "lapsed," that is,
yielded to threats or succumbed to torture and renounced
the faith. Should the lapsed be readmitted to membership
in the Church at all, and if so, on what footing? Must they
not be rebaptized? In North Africa, resistance to persecution had been strong, and the rigorists declined either to
readmit the lapsed or to accept the ministrations of bishops
and priests whose behavior under persecution had not been
above reproach.

There followed disputes over the election of bishops and
over the validity of baptisms and ordinations. The rigorists,
led by Donatus, bishop of Carthage, appealed to Constantine to settle their disputes with their opponents who
claimed to represent the valid hierarchy. Followers of

Donatus attempted to seize the churches of their opponents and to drive out clergy whom they considered to have been dishonored. The Donatists established their own hierarchy and organized their own churches. All this produced major disturbances of public order.

The Arian and Donatist controversies illustrate two types of ecclesiastical disorders with which the government would have to deal because they became public issues, namely heresy, or false doctrine, and schism, or the establishment of a separate church. Both heresy and schism posed political problems. If heresy caused a real division in the Church, and led to the establishment of a separate church, there would be schism, and the unity of faith which was essential to the nature of the Church would be lost. The government was concerned because the security and prosperity of the empire depended on religious harmony within the state. It has been an axiom of Roman statecraft that the safety of the Roman people depended on the good will of the gods of Rome, and the teaching of Christianity made it obvious that God, who would punish individual wrongdoers, would punish a nation that harbored spiritual error. Therefore it was the duty of the Christian emperor to take measures to maintain spiritual truth and harmony among his subjects.

In line with his duty, Constantine introduced two innovations of great moment for both the Church and the government. The emperor, acting on his responsibility for public order, summoned councils of bishops to consider charges of the kind that had been raised by the Arian and Donatist disputes. The police powers of the state were used to enforce the decrees of the councils which found it necessary to depose or exile bishops and priests. The Church welcomed the support of the state without realizing the danger to the independence of the Church that might be inherent in the state's participation in its internal affairs.

The Council of Nicaea, summoned in 325 to deal with the Arian controversy, was a milestone in the history of

Christianity in its new status as an institution within the state. The epoch-making aspects of the council were that it was an ecumenical gathering of bishops summoned by the emperor in his capacity as head of the state; that it formulated an official creed that was to serve not only as a declaration of faith but as a test of orthodoxy; and that its decrees were enforced by the police of the state.

The creed adopted at Nicaea was an attempt to devise a statement concerning the nature of Christ which would provide a proper basis for worship that would also be acceptable to Christians who were attracted by Arius' ideas. The creed stated that Christians believed in Christ who was begotten of the Father, only-begotten, that is, begotten of the same substance as the Father; that he was God out of God, Light out of Light, true God out of true God, of the same substance with the Father.

Objection was vigorously made to the presence in the creed of the Greek term *homoousios*, "of the same substance," which was not a scriptural word, and it is at least doubtful whether the bishops at Nicaea were wholly satisfied that they had reached a permanent settlement of the Arian problem. This council proved to be only the first in a long series in which problems of belief had to be debated, and in which the imperial government often found itself taking sides, and using its influence, or its police power, to settle theological disputes.

But on another level the life of the Church continued in spite of theological controversy. The Church was distinguished from pagan religion in its priesthood. In most of the pagan cults the priests were not trained professionals, whereas one of the strengths of the Church was its organization in a professional hierarchy of trained and disciplined clergy. Under the bishop, who was the chief pastor in each city, priests and deacons, assisted by lay workers, conducted services of worship, gave instruction, and carried out the social and charitable work which was one of the Church's most important functions. In pre-Christian times charitable and educational foundations, social clubs and burial guilds had been active, but normally only on a municipal scale. The Christians were prepared to carry on the same work on a provincial, or ecumenical, scale. The Church built hospitals, orphanages, and homes for old people on a scale that had not existed previously. The only organized work comparable to that of the Church existed in the Jewish communities, but here the difference was that the church offered its services to everyone, Christian and non-Christian alike.

There were a number of ways in which the churches became the centers of community life. The services, of which Holy Communion was the central and essential corporate act, brought the members of the community together on a footing of equality and brotherhood. The preachers offered systematic instruction which could be supplemented by the mosaics and paintings in the churches that depicted scenes of Biblical history. The processions and outdoor festivities at the great seasons of the Church year were occasions for manifestation of the solidarity of the Christian community. The churches in the large cities, and those in the towns and villages to a lesser extent, were surrounded by enclosures containing houses for the clergy, quarters for the schools for choir boys, and facilities for distribution of food and clothing to the poor. A large church would require a considerable staff of clergy for all its activities. Widows were expected to assist in charitable and social work.

Need to raise money for support of its work became a major concern of the Church and indeed was one of the reasons for its acquiring property and becoming active in business enterprises. The office of the patriarch of Alexandria operated a fleet of merchant vessels and applied the profits to its charitable work.

The Church's most important contribution to the Greco-Roman community was its concept of a common basis of membership in a religious community. Stoicism had taught the brotherhood of man, and some of the pagan cults, notably Mithraism, had received on an equal footing initiates of all ranks of society, including slaves. Stoicism, however, was not organized, and Mithraism was a secret cult. Christianity introduced into the stratified society of its day the idea that membership in the community was based on the fatherhood of God and was expressed in the distinctive concept of Christian love. The Church accepted women on an equal basis with men, which was not the case in public life. It did not attempt to abolish slavery, which was an essential part of the economy, but it put forward a new teaching that master and slave were both spiritual heirs of Christ and as such had responsibilities in their conduct toward each other.

The social teaching of Christianity was reflected in the revision of legislation which began with Constantine, in which the laws concerning divorce, the legal status of women and orphans, and the treatment of slaves were made more humane.

The main impact of Christianity was on the urban civilization of the Greco-Roman cities, as was illustrated in the earliest Christian history, the book of the Acts of the Apostles. By the time of the Late Roman Empire the Church had greater resources, but the mission was still an urban one, though it was encountering different kinds of problems and the Church, as a larger and more complex institution, had to devote more of its energy to its internal affairs.

• *The Constantinian Dynasty* When Constantine died (337) it was the first time in many years that an emperor had left sons of his own who could succeed him. This made possible what it was hoped would prove to be a stable dynasty that would perpetuate the control of a family that had already achieved prestige and commanded substantial loyalty. In the Roman world, the family, whether of private persons or public figures, possessed an important meaning as a social and historical unit, and the Constantinian house was unusually fortunate in the existence of three heirs, all of an age to take an active part in the rule of the empire. When Constantine's sons partitioned the empire among themselves as Augusti, it seemed as though the collaboration of three brothers would assure the kind of harmonious sharing of responsibility that had been the aim of the Tetrarchy. Constantine II, the eldest, took as his share Britain, Gaul, and Spain. These were not the most important provinces, but Constantine II seems to have been given, as well, some kind of status of primacy. Constantius became ruler of the eastern provinces, to which Thrace was added. Constans took Italy, Africa, Pannonia, Macedonia, and Dacia.

The rivalry that had caused the failure of the Tetrarchy soon appeared. Constantine II made war on Constans and invaded Italy—to his undoing, for he was killed in battle (340). Constans thus became ruler of two thirds of the empire. Constantius, who had inherited the war with Persia, was for some years occupied with annual campaigns on the Mesopotamian frontier.

Along with the external danger of the rising power of Persia, the brothers had inherited the persistent political problem of Arianism. The creed of orthodoxy promulgated at Nicaea had by no means put an end to the activities of the followers of Arius, who had died in 335. In addition to the dispute between Arians and the orthodox, as to whether Christ was to be considered of the same substance of God (as the Nicene creed stated) or not of the same substance (as the Arians claimed), there was dissension within the orthodox party over the word *homoousios*, "of the same substance," which some bishops would not accept because it was not found in scripture. As a solution, some theologians were willing to accept the term *homoiousios*, "of like substance," but even the bishops who rejected the blasphemous teaching of Arius were troubled over what they considered the unsatisfactory character of the formula of Nicaea.

The division of opinion reached such proportions that Constantius was obliged to take a personal stand. Once more the imperial house was seriously involved in theological politics. Constantius inclined toward Arian ideas, as his father had done in his last years, and used his influence accordingly. In the East, Athanasius, bishop of Alexandria, almost alone fought for the creed of Nicaea. In terms of the bitter theological warfare of those days, it was "Athanasius against the world."

In an age when men's life expectancy was short, by modern standards, the life expectancy of an emperor might be even shorter; few could expect to remain in power for over thirty years, as Constantine the Great had. Constans was assassinated in Gaul in a palace revolution in 350, and an army officer named Magnentius was proclaimed Augustus. Constantius, free for the time being of the Persian war, invaded the West and finally defeated the usurper (353). Sixteen years after the death of Constantine the Great, the empire was again united under one Augustus.

Constantius as sole Augustus was a different person from his father. The contemporary sources indicate that he lacked his father's mental capacity and was not a highly educated person. Perhaps because he realized his shortcomings, he tended to be vain and suspicious. When faced with difficult decisions, he was apt to be timid and easily influenced by the persons who happened to be nearest to him. However, he was an able soldier and a conscientious emperor.

As soon as he was sole emperor, Constantius undertook to put an end to the continuing strife in the Church. His concerns were unity and peace. To achieve this he summoned councils in both East and West which were presided over by high government officials he carefully picked. Constantius regarded Athanasius and the western bishops as responsible for the troubles, and the most conservative leaders of the original Nicene party were deposed and exiled before the creed-making councils were convoked.

Under strong pressure from the government, the councils worked out a creed which avoided using the controversial term "substance," and merely stated that Christ was "like to" God. This attempt at compromise could be accepted by the Nicene party, although with the greatest reluctance because it did not expressly exclude Arian teaching. By its nature this creed was not a theological statement that could be permanent, and it was revised as soon as practicable after Constantius' death.

The emperor's name was not remembered with favor or gratitude by the Church. It had been shown that it was possible for imperial pressure to impose a settlement of a doctrinal dispute which the Church councils, if they had been able to act freely, would not have accepted. An important consequence was that the Constantinian house was identified, in the eyes of both Christians and pagans, with partisan support of a violently controversial issue within the Church.

• *Life and Work in the Christian Empire*   The conversion of Constantine to Christianity came at a time when momentous social and economic changes were already under way. To these were added equally momentous alterations in the structure of the government, and the emergence of the Church as a new institution within the state added a further component, of a kind that had not existed before, to the life of the empire.

Single examples of these changes, with some indication of their immediate causes, have already been mentioned at appropriate points. However, they must be seen in a larger context and against a background that existed before the time of the Late Roman Empire. Viewed in this perspective, they will help to explain certain features of the history of the period as it evolves in the remainder of the study.

Edward Gibbon wrote that one of the reasons for the decline and fall of the Roman empire was its "immoderate greatness," by which he meant its excessive size. His observation emphasizes one aspect of the empire's physical composition that affected all of its history, namely the variety of people that the empire came to embrace, from Syria to Spain and from Egypt to Britain. Caracalla's edict (A.D. 212 or 213), which granted Roman citizenship to virtually all free persons in the empire, had by no means made them all Romans. Roman rule could not have done away with the wide differences in life and work that continued to exist in all its territories after they were acquired by Rome.

The arrival of the Roman conquerors made little essential difference to the artisans and peasants of the provinces. It was normal at that time for the lower classes to be illiterate, or barely literate. What preserved local patterns of life even more significantly was that the common people in the provinces usually spoke only their indigenous languages, such as Punic, Celtic, Syriac, and Coptic. The Romans did not trouble to learn these languages; the natives, if they were ambitious, had to learn Greek or Latin. It would probably not have occurred to the Roman authorities to introduce a system of universal education to teach all their subjects the Latin language and culture as a means of achieving political solidarity. Indeed, it would probably have been physically impossible to do so in the world of that time.

The persistence of native languages illustrates how life and work in the provinces continued on the local level, in contrast to the empire-wide uniformity of Roman administration. The empire was in effect a great common market with excellent roads; internal tolls on goods were not burdensome. However, the evidence indicates that trade between the provinces, while active in some commodities, such as wine, olive oil, and pottery, was not as extensive as it would be in modern times, and that it was not as important in the overall economy as agriculture. Transportation by land was expensive and slow, and commodities as a rule were produced for local consumption. In the cities and towns throughout the empire, independent craftsmen continued to work individually, or in family units, as they had done before the arrival of the Romans, and normally sold their products directly to the consumers. Alongside the craftsmen were small shopkeepers dealing in local products. The state of technology did not permit mass production. The government either manufactured the things it needed, such as arms and uniforms, or ordered its requirements direct from the producers, so that there was little profit for merchants in trade with the government.

Such conditions naturally made it impossible for Roman rule fully to assimilate the people in its many provinces. Another reason why it was impossible to achieve real social integration among the members of the empire as a whole lay in the perpetuation, indeed intensification, of the characteristic Roman stratification of society which had been exported to the provinces along with the Roman administrative system.

Ample evidence attests to the wide gulf between the rich and the poor in both the cities and the country. This gulf was still what it had always been in the prosperous days of the republic and the early empire. Ammianus Marcellinus, the distinguished pagan historian of the fourth century, left vivid pictures of Rome in his day, a great city conspicuous for a luxurious, corrupt, indolent nobility, intent on their own pleasures and on the personal advantages that were to be looked for in politics. Wealth was displayed in every possible form. The rich man in his conspicuous dress, attended by throngs of slaves, gorged himself at magnificent banquets, and cared nothing for the masses he and his friends exploited.

The other side of the picture was the spectacle of the dissolute common people, living on the dole, greedy, violent, and ignorant. The chariot races at the Circus Maximus were the principal excitement of these unlovely people, who otherwise, Ammianus wrote, spent all their lives with wine and dice.

The emperor Julian, himself an accomplished writer, left

a comparable picture of life in Antioch in Syria in the middle of the fourth century. The rich landowners, Julian found when he visited the city, had been openly occupying municipal grazing lands for their own profit; and when a drought caused a local famine, they hoarded their stocks of food to force prices up. If the poor starved, it was not their affair. When Julian imported wheat to relieve the distress, and had bread sold at low fixed prices, it was the poor from the country as well as the poor in the city who flocked to buy it.

Ammianus and Julian took for granted the social, economic, and political framework that produced the evils they saw in Rome and Antioch. They both called for reform, but it was moral reform of the people as individuals, not reform of the social system.

The observations recorded by Ammianus and Julian, which could be paralleled from other sources, illustrate a situation that affected the whole of the history of the Late Roman Empire. When the government of the Late Empire, in order to assure production of food and goods and payment of taxes, tied workers and municipal property owners to their stations, the classes grew more rigid and the barriers between them grew more marked. The rich continued to live as they always had, using their influence to avoid paying their fair share of the cost of the government and at the same time continuing to enrich themselves by obtaining favors from the government and by exploiting the lower classes. Lesser folk had to live more and more just for the sake of their own prescribed tasks and responsibilities. When the government needed more money, it raised taxes though the basis of production was not increased. The effect on morale was obvious.

One of the most striking illustrations of the effects of social stratification is the history of the agricultural problem in the Late Empire. The problem was vital, not only because agriculture was the principal national industry and the source of the largest proportion of the national income, but because any weakness in agriculture inescapably was felt in all other areas of the national life.

In Roman history ownership of land had always been the favorite form of investment for the rich and the aristocracy. Landed estates were a visible token of secure status. But the supply of workers might be a problem. In the prosperous times of the republic and the earlier days of the empire, large estates could be worked by slaves, but by the time of the Late Empire slaves had become scarce and too expensive to be used for agricultural work. The sources tell of small farmers living laborious lives, and existing for the most part on the subsistence level. As a rule they were unable to accumulate any surplus either of money or food. The agricultural methods of the time were such that a comparatively large amount of labor by a number of people was necessary to raise a relatively limited quantity of products. When local famines occurred, as they often did, the expense of transportation made relief difficult and the farmers had to seek help from the landlords or in the cities. In the provinces, their lives were probably not greatly different from those of their forebears under the pre-Roman masters.

Inescapably, independent farmers lived in constant danger of losing their holdings to wealthy landowners when failures of crops made it impossible for them to meet expenses and pay taxes. Free farmers sometimes had to become tenants. Marginal land was constantly going out of cultivation, often in substantial amounts, while the economic and social position of the farmers deteriorated steadily. Farmers in distress tried to leave their land to seek employment, or the dole, in the cities, or to become brigands. In the Late Empire, the free peasants gradually sank to the status of serfs.

The collections of laws of the Late Roman Empire show the agricultural problem as a continual source of concern to the government. Laws had to be repeated enforcing the restrictions on the movement of farmers, while in cases of extreme distress arrears of taxes had to be remitted. Various devices were tried to return abandoned land to cultivation. In time farmers were forbidden to serve in the army—in which they had once been able to find refuge from their troubles—while at the same time the government settled army veterans and barbarian prisoners of war on the land as a means of increasing the agricultural population. The persistence of the problem shows that the government's successive efforts to deal with it were never really effective. It is significant of the depressed state of the workers on the land that they rose in revolt only a few times.

More and more the energies of the middle and lower classes were devoted to the maintenance of the government and the army, whose members were themselves not productive. In fact the army came to be separated from the rest of society. When the sources of recruits inside the empire were no longer adequate, in part because of the way in which workers had to be tied to their occupations, the army had to depend increasingly on hired barbarians. When Roman citizens no longer expected to have to serve as soldiers, the empire lost another common bond of patriotism.

It is against this background of social deterioration that the history of the Late Roman Empire has to be read. In terms of the consequences of its "immoderate greatness," the Roman empire was the victim of its own success.

3 The Christian State Triumphant over Paganism

• *The "New-Old" Century*   The conversion of Constantine and the emancipation of the Church created problems —political, social, and intellectual as well as religious— which could only be worked out gradually. The fourth century was an era in which two schemes of life, classical and Christian, old and new, came together, and out of the tension and struggle of this confrontation came a new Christian Roman Empire in which the traditions of the old empire were absorbed and transformed.

This chapter deals with three main facets of the empire's history during this crucial period of conflict. First, the brief but eventful reign of the emperor Julian illustrates the comprehensive character of the reaction in pagan circles to the policies of Constantine and his sons. Second, the chapter describes the processes by which the Church, now a public institution, established itself not only as a religious power but as a social, intellectual, and educational force in the community. This growth in scope of the Church's life was paralleled by the skillful efforts of the spokesmen for classical culture, who endeavored to show that the ancient religious and intellectual tradition was superior to Christianity. In the process of this confrontation, Christian thinkers completed the harmonization of classical thought and Christian theology which became the foundation for Christian society and intellectual life.

Finally, the chapter deals with the Church's share in

creating its place in the new political climate. Here two forceful figures—Bishop Ambrose of Milan and Emperor Theodosius I—effected an important advance in the status of the Church, bringing to decision political questions that had been raised by the conversion of Constantine but not settled at that time. It was now officially declared that the Church was a state church.

• *The Emperor Julian and the Reaction Against the Constantinian House* When Constantius became sole Augustus in 353, the last remaining members of the Constantinian house were his younger cousins Gallus and Julian, the latter a bookish young man who had not been given a role in public affairs. Constantius appointed Gallus Caesar of the East, but the appointment was far from a success. Gallus, cruel and ignorant, conducted himself so outrageously that Constantius was forced to have him executed.

Constantius, again sole ruler, was desperately in need of assistance in Gaul, which was threatened with invasion by the German tribes from beyond the Rhine. Preservation of the dynasty was important, and although Gallus' half brother Julian was considered a dreamer, Constantinian blood counted. Constantius appointed Julian to the rank of Caesar in 355, expecting to be able to control him through his staff, and placed him in charge of the operations in Gaul.

Astonishingly, the young intellectual proved an able general and a capable administrator. In time there was reason to fear that the emperor looked upon Julian as a dangerous rival. The fate of Gallus was an example, and in 360, in an openly hostile act, Julian's troops proclaimed him emperor. An attempt was made at negotiation, but Julian thought it safer to try to force a settlement. Emperor and Caesar moved against each other but en route Constantius died suddenly (361). His last act, for the sake of the dynasty, was to designate Julian as his successor.

The Emperor Julian. Marble statue in the Louvre, Paris. (*Hirmer Verlag, Munich*)

The new emperor created a sensation when he let it be known that he had, some time before, secretly renounced Christianity and embraced the ancient pagan religion. Suddenly the empire found that Christianity was no longer the religion supported by the reigning dynasty. This was a reversal matching in political consequences the conversion of Constantine a half-century earlier.

Julian "the Apostate" has come down in history as a tragic figure who fought heroically for restoration of the ancient gods until his premature death in battle in Persia after a reign of only twenty months. Julian's career was brief but important in the history of the Late Roman Empire because it shows that the conflict between paganism and Christianity was not simply religious and emotional. His program was not wholly directed at the revival of pagan religion and the suppression of Christianity. The religious program was conspicuous, but in reality Julian worked to eliminate many features of the political and economic policies of the Constantinian house which he and his peers looked upon as evils to be corrected.

There was indeed need for reform. The ambitious building program of Constantine the Great and Constantius had been costly, and military expenses had been heavy in the war against Persia under the two emperors as well as in operations against the usurper Magnentius in Gaul. The government had sought to meet its extraordinary expenses by inflation of the currency, which, as always, was hardest on the middle and lower classes. One of Julian's first measures was reform of the currency.

The municipalities were harder pressed than ever by the government's demands for taxes and services. In many cities Julian found that taxes were so badly in arrears that the arrears had to be remitted. The leading citizens, compelled by law to serve in the local senates, were being ruined. Some members of the local aristocracies refrained from marrying so that they would not have to pass on their burdens to their heirs, and lived with concubines, whose children, being illegitimate, could not inherit their fathers' status and duties. Julian also discovered that some prosperous citizens were not serving in their local senates as they should have been, and he ordered them forcibly enrolled.

Like the government in general, the imperial court was heavily overstaffed. Julian, by this time an experienced administrator, began to work at the reorganization of the central administration and purged the court of superfluous functionaries and army officers whose duties were purely decorative. The savings in expense were considerable.

Another area badly in need of attention was the administration of justice. Under the autocratic regime of Constantine and his sons there had been many complaints that the common people were deprived of legal assistance and the means of appeal. Julian undertook to play a more active role than his predecessors in judicial affairs.

Julian's professed aim was to return so far as possible to the less authoritarian administration of the imperial office of the earlier Principate. His comprehensive program showed that he thought of himself as the champion of the common people. In the minds of Julian and his friends, the abandonment of the worship of the traditional gods of Rome could only lead to disaster. The gods would surely punish the Roman people for their neglect. To pagans like Julian, Christianity was a "religion of bad citizenship" which taught men to neglect the religious duties of Roman citizens. From the point of view of traditional Roman statecraft, Christians had always seemed to be atheists who had deserted the religion of their state and society for a strange cult. People like this could not properly form a part of the Roman community.

The basic need to prepare citizens for their duties involved reform of the educational program. Julian's edict on the qualifications of teachers was one of his most characteristic measures, and one of the most controversial. Christian teachers, the edict declared, must not be allowed to teach the pagan classics, which were the core of the traditional curriculum. It was intellectually dishonest for a teacher to teach a subject he not only did not believe in but believed to be wrong. Moreover, a Christian teacher, offering instruction in the classical writings, would be able by his method of presentation to corrupt the minds of his students. Therefore, the decree provided, Christians must henceforth teach only Christian subject matter. In spite of the protests that were raised by pagans as well as Christians, the decree actually represented a logical part of Julian's program. The edict must have been ignored or repealed after Julian's death, for nothing further is heard of it.

Julian's efforts for the revival of pagan worship did not meet with the enthusiastic support he had confidently expected. Many pagans had become lax in their private worship and indifferent to the public worship that Julian believed was important not only as an expression of true religious feeling but as a symbol of the ancient intellectual origins of the Greco-Roman world.

What the future course of Julian's religious campaign would have been had he lived is a question that cannot be answered. Believing that he had an opportunity to overthrow the king of Persia and replace him with the king's refugee brother who was serving as an officer in the Roman army, Julian set out for the Persian front and was killed while fighting in Mesopotamia (363). He left no heir, and the house of Constantine came to an end with him. The day following Julian's death a Christian officer of the imperial guard named Jovian was chosen emperor, and a hasty and disgraceful peace was purchased from Persia.

Julian's brief career illustrated one of the forms that the clash between paganism and Christianity might take. In this case the clash originated on the highest level of the imperial administration, but there were other ways in which the confrontation was maintained. Here again the encounter was not wholly religious but involved the competition of two intellectual, social, and political systems that were essentially different in kind.

• *Paganism and Christianity at Court and in the Cities*
When the emperor Constantine was converted to the new religion, a number of prominent civil and military officials remained pagans. Constantine and some of his successors had to continue to work with a recognizable group of officials who personally did not accept the new faith that had the official protection of the sovereign. Some influential pagans hoped that it would be possible to induce the emperor to put away the strange un-Roman cult and return to the proper worship of the Roman gods. The pagan party at court was led by the distinguished Greek philosopher Sopater. The arguments these apologists employed illustrate the effect on statecraft of the simultaneous existence of paganism and Christianity.

One of the leading successors of Sopater was a well-known orator and teacher in Constantinople, Themistius, who gained a recognized position at court because of his eloquence and his success as a teacher of rhetoric and philosophy. Under the Christian regime, down to the end of the century, he pursued a successful career and was appointed governor of Constantinople and tutor to one of the sons of the emperor Theodosius I.

Themistius made good use of his opportunity to serve as a spokesman for the classical tradition. A person in his position was expected to present congratulatory addresses to the emperors on their accession and on important official anniversaries. In these addresses Themistius took care not to attack Christianity directly. His method was to imply, without mentioning Christianity, that the classical religious and intellectual tradition offered everything in the way of moral instruction and preparation for public service that

Christianity offered. Likewise he reminded each emperor that the ideal qualities of the Roman ruler—justice, wisdom, clemency, devotion to duty, and so on—had all been developed and exemplified in the emperors of the first centuries of the historic empire.

Themistius performed an important service to the pagan cause by demonstrating in his own person that the classical tradition could produce a man of letters and courtier whom the Christian emperors could welcome and respect. His career shows that the Christian rulers, even while they were engaged in active measures for the suppression of pagan rites, found it desirable to maintain good relations with a distinguished pagan at court.

Beyond Constantinople were the great cities of the empire. The Greco-Roman world was a world of cities, each with its history, its distinctive social tradition, its intellectual life. The action of Christianity on the cities and of the cities on Christianity, first described in the Acts of the Apostles, continued throughout the Late Roman Empire. Constantinople was a new Christian foundation and did not have a history extending back into the classical era such as the older cities possessed. In the encounter of Christianity and classicism in these older cities may be seen the nature of the forces that determined the history and culture of the new Christian empire. Rome and Antioch are two of these cities for which a substantial amount of literary evidence has been preserved.

Antioch had a special history. While it was so well known as a home of the classical tradition that the emperor Julian made it the main center for his program, it had also been the famous headquarters of the early Christian mission to the gentiles and took pride in having been the place where the disciples were first called "Christians." The careers of the emperor Julian and of Themistius illustrate two ways in which paganism could attempt to deal with Christianity; a third way is illustrated in the career of Libanius of Antioch, the distinguished orator who became one of the leading personages in the city in the middle and latter part of the fourth century.

Antioch, like all the Greek cities of the eastern provinces of the empire, retained its original Greek culture under Roman occupation, and Libanius in his teaching and public service devoted himself to perpetuation of the social and intellectual ideals of the classical Greek *polis*. His success as a teacher brought him pupils from all over the world, and Libanius could with justice point to the effectiveness of the ancient Hellenic education as demonstrated by the successful careers of many of his former students in the law, the civil service, and the imperial administration. The high level of the social and intellectual life of Antioch, Libanius took pleasure in pointing out, was possible only because the city remained true to the educational and social patterns of the ancient Greek city. Libanius acknowledged the existence of Christianity but did not engage in polemic.

What Libanius could not acknowledge was that Antioch had become a great Christian city. In recognition of its role in the apostolic mission, Constantine the Great had presented Antioch with a church which, because of its magnificence and its gilded roof tiles, was called the Golden Church. The bishops of Antioch enjoyed the special position that was the right of the occupants of the sees that had been founded by apostles—Jerusalem, Antioch, Alexandria, and Rome (in the case of Antioch, Peter).

In addition, Antioch in the fourth century had the distinction of producing one of the greatest preachers in the history of the Church, St. John Chrysostom, "John of the Golden Tongue." As a youth he was a pupil of Libanius and followed the traditional curriculum of Greek classical literature. Later John employed his natural literary talent as an instrument of his remarkable gifts as teacher and pastor. The work of Libanius and John Chrysostom illustrates the way in which paganism and Christianity found themselves living side by side in the great cities. When there was an insurrection in Antioch in 387 caused by imposition by the government of an emergency tax of heavy proportions, Libanius and Chrysostom were the leading spokesmen of the two communities within the city.

The career of John Chrysostom exemplifies the mission of the Church in the great urban centers. His treatise *On the Priesthood* describes all the aspects of the priest's vocation —his role as minister of the sacraments, visitor of the sick and widows, teacher, and organizer of relief for the poor. Chrysostom writes of the problems the parish priest must be prepared to deal with—the sick who are absorbed with their own ailments, widows who love to gossip, well-to-do parishioners who do not give as much money as they should. Chrysostom noted that when food and clothing were being distributed to the poor, deacons should stand by and watch the lines to prevent certain persons from passing through the line twice.

• *The Church and Classical Culture* While the Church in its new freedom was building up its day-by-day mission in the world, scholars of the Church were busy with the problem of bringing the Church into its rightful place in the intellectual life of the empire. In its earliest days the Church had been separated, religiously, socially, and intellectually, from what Christians spoke of as "the world." The earliest believers regarded Greek philosophy as "vain deceit"; classical literature was considered unsuitable for Christian readers because of its immoral tone. At the same time, pagans, whose education had been the traditional curriculum of the masterpieces of literature and philosophy, were unable to accept Christian doctrine because the writers of the Christian scriptures were obviously not educated men; because they were uneducated, their mental ability was questionable and their writings could not carry authority.

The situation changed as educated pagans began to be converted in mature years. In the second and third centuries the Christian philosophers of Alexandria, Clement and Origen, following the thought of the Hellenized Jew Philo, perceived that there were aspects of classical philosophy and ethics, especially in the thought of Plato (whom some Christian writers spoke of as "our Plato"), that came close to Christian teaching. These aspects of classical thought, they showed, had an intrinsic value as studies of human morality, and the Christian philosophers now set out to adapt the best elements of classical philosophy to Christian thought. Christian apologists began to be able to present Christian doctrine in a style that educated pagans could listen to.

In both East and West the century produced leading theologians who were also distinguished men of letters. In the East, Basil the Great, his brother Gregory of Nyssa, and their cousin Gregory of Nazianzus put the vocabulary and methods of Greek philosophy at the service of theology, and developed a Christian psychology and anthropology. In addition, Gregory of Nazianzus wrote sensitive poetry.

In the West, the careers of Ambrose and Jerome illustrate the way in which both the Roman tradition of public administration and the tradition of Latin literature and rhetoric made their contribution to the development of Christian society. Ambrose, a member of a noble family, began to follow a career of government service; then, while a provincial governor resident at Milan, he was suddenly, in 374, elected bishop of the city by the local factions of both orthodox and Arians. Ambrose exhibited the many-sided talents, both practical and literary, often found among the Roman nobility. His vigorous defense of the claims of the church in face of the secular authority will be discussed later in this chapter. He preached to crowds and fought pagans, Arians, and other heretics. At the same time, he kept up voluminous theological and literary activity. He put into Latin form the current dogmatic thought of the Greek fathers, and produced moral and ascetic treatises of his own, as well as handbooks on the priesthood and hymns.

Jerome, who likewise came of a wealthy family and was

educated under famous teachers, exemplifies another type
of service to the Church and to Christian society in which
the instinct of the true man of letters was combined—not
always peacefully for Jerome—with the desire for the ascetic life and the urgent summons to theological combat.
Jerome learned Greek and Hebrew, collected a considerable library, compiled studies of Church history and biogra-
phy, and produced the so-called Vulgate translation of the
Bible. All the while he continued to study his beloved classical authors, and he expounded their works, for thirty-four
years, in his monastic school in Bethlehem. His letters—
which were always designed for eventual publication—
preserve a remarkable record of an active and many-sided
mind and of contemporary pagan and Christian society.

• *The Ascetic Movement* While the Church had been
creating the new Christian community in the cities, towns,
and villages, another branch of the Christian community
was coming into being on another plane. The ascetic call-
ing, a characteristic phenomenon of the Late Roman Empire, was not new with Christianity. There had been ascetics in the classical world, such as Diogenes the Cynic, a
philosopher who lived in a barrel, and Indian fakirs had
visited Athens and Rome. What was new in Christian ascet-
icism was the source of the motivation.

Renunciation of the world by the solitary ascetic and by
the monk living in a religious community might represent
several different impulses. To some Christians, from the
Church's earliest days, the flesh, with its frailty and tempta-
tions, became abhorrent; lust had to be overcome before
man could partake fully of the joys of Christianity. This
impulse might lead to excessive mortification of the flesh—
even to eccentricities such as living on the tops of pillars or
in trees, which the Church disapproved but could not very
well stop completely. In many cases, denial of self and
mortification of the body represented the same passionate
desire to give one's life for the sake of the Lord that in the

early days of the Church had compelled many Christians to welcome martyrdom. With persecution ended after the emancipation of the Church, a man who earlier might have been a martyr became a monk.

Other Christians, especially in the early period of the Church's freedom, withdrew into solitude because they disapproved of the way in which the Church was acquiring worldly interests and material wealth, to the detriment, they considered, of its spiritual life. Still others withdrew from the distractions of the world to free themselves for contemplation and prayer. This was the most constructive form of the ascetic life. Some young men, for example John Chrysostom, retired for some years to the desert or to a mountain cave in order to achieve self-denial in preparation for the active ministry. Others attempted to use the ascetic life as a refuge from the burdens of taxation, compulsory public service, and military obligations.

In the early fourth century the monastic communities were founded which became so influential in the life of the Church and of Christian society. The monks, spending their time in prayer and labor, sought a spiritual perfection which they believed was not possible for persons living in the world. Christianity, like Platonism, taught that there were two worlds, the visible world of material things and the invisible world of the spirit, which was in fact the true world. The lives of the ascetics represented, for them, not an escape from reality but an escape into reality. Often these holy men became spiritual advisers to lay people who came to consult them. Their life constituted prayer for the whole Christian community. The celebrated desert solitary St. Anthony became the champion of the faith in Egypt and the national hero. Many monasteries rescued orphans and conducted schools and hospitals. Monks served as physicians and nurses in the army.

In any such system there could be abuses. Wandering monks, not living under discipline, roamed the countryside begging for food or, as nonbelievers said, stealing. Groups of monks not attached to regular establishments lived in cities and made a pleasant vocation of ministering to fashionable ladies. Some monks were illiterate or had only the lowest level of education, but this was true also of many people in the world. What was regarded as the idleness of the monks, and the eccentricities of some, brought the ascetic life into disrepute. But the ascetic movement was a natural development of the times, sociologically as well as religiously, and in spite of abuse it maintained a tradition of otherworldliness that lent strength to the Church.

• *Theodosius, the State Church, and Pagan Society* Julian's reign had thoroughly alarmed the Church and had taught its leaders the wisdom of trying to patch up their quarrels. After his death, however, theological warfare continued over the problem of the definition of the nature of Christ, and the government continued to be confronted with the resulting public disorders. Experience had indicated that official intervention on one side or the other would inevitably produce new troubles, and for the time being at least, Julian's successor Jovian (363–364) and Jovian's successors, the colleagues Valentinian I (364–375) and his brother Valens (364–378), found it prudent to issue official declarations of toleration of both paganism and Christianity in all its sects.

However, the attitude of the government vis-à-vis the Church depended in great measure on the personal religious inclination of the ruler of the moment. Valentinian I and Valens were both devoted Christians but their temperaments differed. Valentinian, as ruler of the western half of the empire, respected the principle of toleration, but Valens, in the East, while he maintained the toleration of paganism, considered it his duty to enforce orthodoxy among Christians.

At this time official orthodoxy was the creed which Constantius had forced on the Church and which stopped short

of excluding Arian doctrine. Adherents of the traditional
Nicene faith could not accept this formula because its statement of the nature of Christ did not satisfy them. Thus
Valens was required by theological logic to persecute the
followers of the Nicene faith, which he proceeded to do
with great vigor. Once more a question of belief became a
public issue. The partisans of the theological factions
fought in the streets, bishops were exiled, and control of
churches was bitterly contested. Sometimes a city had two
rival bishops, one "orthodox," supported by the government, and one "heretical," followed with passionate devotion by his flock. An Arian woman killed a Nicene bishop.

Valens' career came to an inglorious end. Goths who had
been admitted to the eastern lands of the empire in the
hope of relieving the shortage of manpower in the Roman
army were so shamefully mistreated by some Roman officials that they rebelled. Valens met them with his forces at
Adrianople (378). The Goths won a resounding victory and
Valens was killed. The empire again was in danger. Since
Valentinian was already dead, his son and successor Gratian (375–383), now seventeen years old, chose as his colleague Theodosius, a distinguished general of Spanish
origin, and placed him in command of the East.

Theodosius' reign (379–395) opened a major epoch in
the history of the Late Roman Empire. He had as colleagues in the West the youthful Gratian, and after his
death Gratian's half-brother Valentinian II (383–392), but
Theodosius was always the dominant figure and operated
both in West and East as occasion demanded.

Theodosius was a competent ruler, a serious person, and
a deeply religious Christian. He was the first emperor who
did not take the traditional title *pontifex maximus*. From
the beginning of his reign he was determined to make
Christianity a state religion in more specific terms than
Constantine and his successors had been able to achieve. In
February 380, he issued the famous edict in which he de-

clared that all his subjects must adhere to the orthodox
Christian faith, that is, they were to recognize the nature of
the Trinity as composed of Father, Son, and Holy Spirit. All
who did not were heretics and were to incur the severe legal
disabilities appropriate to their crime. Their places of meeting were not entitled to the legal status of churches. They
were subject to punishment on two levels. God would take
vengeance on them, and the government would follow with
its own means of punishment.

The terms of this edict were reinforced by another decree
the following January. The faith of Nicaea was to be respected everywhere. To make the meaning of this plain, the
edict summarized the articles of the Nicene Creed. Heretics
were not to be allowed to call themselves Christians; their
churches were to be given to the Nicene orthodox; and they
were to be driven out of the cities.

These edicts represented, first, a new attempt to settle the
Arian controversy and its ramifications, and second, a step
forward in the legal status of the Church, in that orthodoxy
was now defined and protected by law and heresy became a
crime against the state—that is, a crime against the Roman
people. Theodosius' religious policy was a counterpart to
that of Diocletian a century earlier. Theodosius considered
the persecution of heretics to be necessary to the security of
the state for the same reason that Diocletian had persecuted
Christians. It is difficult to decide whether Theodosius' religious zeal was a reflection of his Spanish origin or whether
he was acting under the forceful guidance of Bishop
Ambrose of Milan.

Paganism was Theodosius' next target. Not only private
worship of the gods, but astrology, magic, divination, and
the oriental cults were still active. Each of these varieties of
belief offered special dangers to Christianity. Especially in
the West, the worship of the oriental god Mithra was a vital
force, its teaching and rites able to win from its initiates a
moral exaltation and spiritual devotion equal in intensity
to the spirituality of Christianity.

It was astrology and the other occult arts that called forth Theodosius' first edict against paganism, in December 381. This law forbade pagan rites intended to foretell the future and prohibited visits to temples for the consultation of oracles. The law was an acknowledgment of the influence that the occult had always possessed in the Greco-Roman world, among persons of all degrees of education and in every level of society. The masters of the occult arts were often invited to practice their skill in the great houses of the nobility. Legislation against astrologers and religious quacks had appeared regularly, but it was impossible to root out the fascination of their lore.

While the occult constituted one kind of threat to the good order of society, the continued vitality of the higher levels of the old religion presented another type of problem to the authorities, for here there was political danger and a real question of loyalty to the state. In the highest circles of society, the members of the old nobility, as always conservative in their ideas and well-grounded in the traditional literary education, carefully preserved the old religion, which to them represented not only a system of spiritual and ethical belief but an intellectual tradition and an expression of patriotic feeling. Worship of the gods was inseparably linked with the historical tradition of Rome's faith in the favor of the special deities of Rome.

As could have been expected, the edict of 381 provoked a strong reaction in the Senates of Rome and Constantinople, both of which included influential adherents of the ancient religion. The Senate of Constantinople obtained a ruling that temples which members of the public were accustomed to visit, not with religious intention, but in order to admire works of art, should not be closed.

In the West there was an even stronger reaction. The senatorial aristocracy of Rome, strongly pagan in composition, felt that even under the Christian regime it preserved the whole of the traditions of ancient Rome—historical, religious, and literary—in a way that the Senate of Con-

stantinople (which to an old Roman was an artificial creation) could not.

The leading figures of the Roman senatorial nobility
were wealthy, highly educated, and devoted to the traditions of family and state. It was characteristic of the times
that the pagan aristocrats were on good terms personally
with those of their peers who were Christians, and that even
in the same family there could be Christians and pagans.
There were some, too, to whom their religion, whether classical or Christian, was a cold and perfunctory thing; but the
differences between Christians and pagans were essentially
deep-seated and on occasion could burst into bitter conflict.

The leaders of the pagan aristocracy in Rome at this time
were men of varied talents. The acknowledged head of the
nobility, Q. Aurelius Symmachus, a distinguished public
servant, well-known through the surviving collection of his
letters, was the chief defender of the pagan religion in its
final fight for toleration. His literary work was judged to
reach the highest standards of the Roman tradition and his
colleagues in the Senate regarded him as their greatest
orator.

A public figure who exemplified another aspect of the
pagan tradition was Vettius Agorius Praetextatus, prefect of
the city, and an elegant man of letters who held many of
the traditional priesthoods. The cult of Vesta, one of the
most ancient symbols of Roman tradition, still survived,
and the pagan senators and their wives carefully maintained the old rites. The cult of the goddess Roma still
commanded enthusiastic devotion. The old forms of religion were not simply a romantic anachronism; the prosperity of the Roman people depended on the worship of the
gods, and the security of the state was involved.

Men of letters shared in the preservation of the classical
tradition. The poet Claudian, much in favor with the
Roman Senate, wrote of a literary paganism and of the
majesty of the city of Rome which the upstart Constantinople could never supplant, while Rutilius Namatianus, of

the provincial aristocracy of Gaul, showed a more spiritual gift in his poems.

The same literary tradition that furnished the pagan men of letters their language and their technique produced eminent Christian poets and scholars. Prudentius, who has been called a Christian Horace as well as a Christian Vergil and Lucretius, wrote the first Christian allegorical epic, as well as famous hymns. Ausonius of Bordeaux, a Christian humanist, wrote as a devotee of the ancient Muses.

The political potential still latent in the conflict between Christianity and paganism erupted in Rome in 382 in the celebrated episode centering around the altar of Victory in the Senate chamber. This was the altar of Victory on which, since the time of Augustus, the members of the Senate had offered sacrifice at the opening of each session. The emperor Constantius, on his visit to Rome in 357, had ordered the altar removed. The order was carried out, but significantly the altar was not destroyed; it was stored, and after the emperor's departure replaced.

Then, when Theodosius' campaign against pagan rites was launched, the youthful emperor Gratian, acting apparently at the prompting of Pope Damasus, ordered the altar removed once more (382). When the pagan members of the Senate petitioned for restoration of the altar, Bishop Ambrose secured a counterpetition of Christian senators and by his personal ascendancy was able to compel Gratian to abide by his original decision. After Gratian's death in the following year the pagan senators organized another petition to the remaining emperor in the West, Valentinian II, who, only thirteen, was under the regency of his mother. The senators' request was a classic statement of the desire of the Roman aristocracy to see maintained the official religious rites that had for so long assured the prosperity of Rome. Different forms of religion, they declared, must be accepted and respected. As the pagan apologists had constantly argued, the senators declared that it was possible to arrive at religious truth by more than one road. In more

practical terms, the petition pointed out that the poor har-
vests in Italy in 383 could be attributed to the wrath of the
slighted gods.

Bishop Ambrose in reply called for freedom of conscience, asserting that it was unfair to compel Christian
senators to meet in the presence of a pagan altar. He
threatened the emperor with excommunication if he
granted the petition, and the petition was rejected. The
whole transaction, beginning with a demonstration of the
strength that paganism still possessed among the members
of the Roman aristocracy, showed what power the Church
could exhibit in the person of an energetic bishop such as
Ambrose.

Indeed a famous clash between the bishop and the emperor a few years later again illustrated the difficult position of the sovereign, personally and officially, in respect to
the authority of the Church. Bishop Ambrose took every
occasion to uphold the Church against the civil power. In
388, Christian monks at Callinicum in Mesopotamia incited
a mob of Christians to burn a synagogue and a chapel of
Christian heretics. Since the Jewish religion was officially
protected, the mob's violence must be punished. When
Theodosius ordered the bishop of Callinicum to rebuild the
synagogue, Bishop Ambrose delivered a sermon in the
presence of the emperor in which he criticized Theodosius'
order and attacked the Jews. The emperor pointed out that
this was not the only occasion on which monks had com-
mitted civil crimes; but when the bishop threatened him
with excommunication, he gave way and promised amnesty
to the rioters.

Two years later the famous episode of the massacre at
Thessalonica occurred. A law issued in the spring of 390
prescribed the death penalty for men guilty of unnatural
vice. Under this law, the military commander at Thessalonica imprisoned a popular charioteer who had seduced a
handsome boy. A mob, indignant at this treatment of their
favorite chariot racer, murdered the military commander

and some members of his staff. Since imperial officials were considered to be personal representatives of the emperor, the murder of a high officer by a city mob was a serious crime amounting to treason.

It was customary on such occasions for a whole city to be punished. Theodosius issued an order to assemble the people of Thessalonica in the circus, where they were systematically slaughtered. In a massacre which lasted seven hours, it is recorded that three thousand people were killed. Theodosius, realizing that his order was excessive, revoked it, but not in time to prevent the killing. Bishop Ambrose wrote Theodosius with his own hand a private letter informing him that he could not be admitted to Holy Communion until he had done penance in the form prescribed by the Church for those guilty of a sin of this kind. Though precisely what followed is not recorded, the emperor must have done penance in satisfactory fashion, as he was admitted to communion the following Christmas.

The celebrated story of the bishop shutting the door of the church in the emperor's face is an apocryphal embellishment which rests on no good evidence. The emperor would not have attempted to enter the church while not authorized to do so, and the bishop would not have shut him out in the manner alleged. The consequences of such action on the part of either would have been incalculable. Ambrose in his funeral sermon on Theodosius' death praised the emperor's high qualities and his services to the Church. But Ambrose had established the principle that (as he expressed it in a letter to the emperor Valentinian II) "the emperor is in the church, not above the church, and the good emperor does not spurn the assistance of the church; he seeks it." Was there any greater honor, the bishop asked, than for the emperor to be called a son of the Church? The bishop's success in his dealings with the emperor set an example that later prelates remembered with good effect.

Though some scholars have questioned whether he is entitled to the epithet "the Great," Theodosius I left his mark on church and state. He finished work that Constantine had set on foot but had not been able to complete. The Church was now definitively established as a state church, and the emperor had declared the state's role in his legislation concerning the Church. With these milestones established, it remained for Justinian to complete the process out of which the Christian Roman Empire emerged in its final form. But in the interval between the reigns of Theodosius I and Justinian the state suffered some profound changes.

4 The Problems
of the Fifth Century
and the Decline of the West

• *The Empire Divided* With the fifth century a new chapter in the history of the empire opens. After Theodosius' death (395) the empire was in effect divided into two halves, eastern and western, Greek and Latin. Often acting independently of each other, sometimes unable to lend each other support when needed, the two halves began to follow different lines of development, which brought them, by the end of the century, to quite different situations. The barbarian nations, which had always been a threat on the boundaries of Rome, now succeeded in breaking into the western empire and by the third quarter of the century made themselves its masters. The eastern half, more fortunate and more prosperous, was able to maintain its integrity, and by the end of the century was on the threshold of the great reign of Justinian.

• *The Empire and the Barbarians* Theodosius' plan to divide the empire between his sons Honorius, who was to be emperor in the West (395–423), and Arcadius, who was to reign in the East (395–408), assumed that the two would act in effective collaboration and that the presence in each half of a ruling Augustus would promote efficiency and security. Dynastic continuity was in effect preserved; grandsons of Theodosius I ruled in both halves of the empire,

Valentinian III in the West (425–455) and Theodosius II in the East (408–450).

Unfortunately, however, the sons and grandsons of Theodosius I did not inherit his ability, and the actual direction of affairs came into the hands of generals and ministers. A significant difference between East and West appeared at once. In the West the men who guided the administration, down to the end of Roman rule there, were almost all generals. In the East civil officials were in charge, while military figures had less influence.

At the same time, in a major change in the traditional character of the Roman administration, German army officers began to come into positions of power in both military and civil affairs. This was a symptom of the massive influx of barbarians into Roman territory which eventually resulted in a profound alteration of the character of the empire. Since the earliest days of Rome, the warlike barbarian tribes beyond the borders had constituted a military threat which varied in intensity at different periods. Eventually the basic task of defense became the holding of the natural frontiers of the Rhine, the Danube, and the Euphrates—a formidable military problem which, as has been seen, was one of the underlying factors in the crisis of the third century. The creation by Diocletian and Constantine of a mobile field army ready to reinforce the garrison troops when an attack came strengthened the defenses, but the Roman army throughout its history had never actually been large enough to defend all the frontiers at once. The barbarian nations were often at war among themselves, and the Romans, when they could, promoted this discord. An official panegyrist of one of the tetrarchs mentioned as barbarian peoples who at that time were active outside the empire Moors, Goths, Burgundians, Alamanni, Vandals, Gepids, Saci, Blemyes, Ethiopians, and other smaller nations. The Alans and Huns had not yet arrived.

By the time of Theodosius I the problem had become acute once more, for two reasons. First, the Germanic tribes then living beyond the frontiers found themselves under heavy pressure from the Huns, who were beginning to move west from the plains of southern Russia. The first result of this, as has been seen, was the admission of Goths into Thrace by Theodosius I.

The second reason lay with the empire's military resources. The pressure of the Germans along the Rhine and the Danube could not be met successfully because the Roman army lacked the necessary manpower. While the army had never been large enough to defend all the frontiers, there is some reason to believe that in the time of Theodosius I there was an actual shortage of men for the army. Whether such a shortage represented an absolute shrinkage of population, caused by a decline in agricultural production which reduced the supply of recruits, or whether the shortage was caused by the growth of the administration, the Church, and the army itself, the preserved sources do not make clear.

The need had to be met by employing barbarians. As far back as the time of Julius Caesar the Romans had employed non-Roman troops to serve as auxiliaries under their own officers, but in the Late Roman Empire, under mounting pressure for soldiers, the practice was vastly extended and the native commanders attained much higher rank and power than in earlier times.

From the time of Theodosius I, when barbarian troops were employed in numbers and permitted to retain their national identity, their presence in the empire brought grave problems to both East and West; for the West the consequences ultimately were disastrous. Barbarians drawn from both inside and outside the empire—Goths, Huns, Alans, Franks, Alamanni—are mentioned in the accounts of the campaigns of Theodosius I and his successors. Those from outside were obtained by treaty or in return for payment of subsidies. The leading generals in West and East at this period have German names: Bauto, Arbogast, Richimer, Hellebich. The ablest assistant of Theodosius I was the Vandal general Stilicho, who at the emperor's death succeeded in making himself the leading power in the West under Honorius and was overthrown only in 408 by the intrigue of a rival.

The employment of barbarian troops did not impair the effectiveness of the army itself, but the political effect of their presence was harmful. The personal success of the German officers and the power they possessed through their control of their own troops created severe friction with the Roman troops and the Roman population. The Roman senators and officials were alarmed for the future of the empire. One incident is typical: in 399 the energetic pursuit of personal power by the Gothic general Gainas, in the service of Arcadius, resulted in a popular uprising in Constantinople in which the Goths in the capital were massacred.

The existence of separate administrations in East and West provided opportunities for an unscrupulous barbarian general, backed by his followers, to blackmail and play one administration against the other. The barbarian generals knew how urgently the services of their people were needed, and when they saw the right occasion, they demanded extra payment in the form of subsidies, threatening to plunder a province or march on one of the capitals if their demands were not satisfied. Sometimes the barbarian general's price would be appointment to a high command.

The last years of the fourth century and the early part of the fifth were filled with such episodes. The notorious career of Alaric, the king of the Visigoths, affords the best-known instances. Alaric found fruitful opportunities in the friction between the eastern and western administrations caused by the ambitious schemes of Stilicho. This energetic general, not satisfied with having become the real power in the West, set out to extend his ascendancy over Arcadius and the eastern government. At this time Alaric had been settled with his people in northern Thrace, from which he was in a position to threaten Constantinople. He took advantage of the eastern government's preoccupation with

Stilicho's plans and began to plunder Thrace, but when he began to march into Greece he was stopped by Stilicho with the combined armies of East and West.

Alaric then persuaded the government in Constantinople to give him command of Illyricum in order to prevent Stilicho from establishing himself there. This gave Alaric a chance to build up his forces and equip them with Roman arms, also to plunder the Macedonian and Dacian provinces. Then, when this territory provided no more booty, Alaric turned to the West. He marched into Italy and besieged the rich city of Milan, while Rome was turned into a fortress by remodeling the wall built by the emperor Aurelian.

Alaric was driven back by Stilicho, but a few years later he found another opportunity in a plan that Stilicho was making to invade Macedonia and Dacia. Alaric now offered his services to Stilicho and they were accepted; but when Stilicho's plan had to be put off because of a massive barbarian invasion, Alaric began to blackmail the government in Rome, in effect demanding money as the price of abstaining from invasion of Italy and an assault on Rome itself.

This demand was met, but after the fall of Stilicho (408) Alaric blockaded the capital and had to be bought off at a high price. The following year, when Alaric was unsuccessful in further demands on Honorius, he again besieged the capital and this time forced the Senate to elect an emperor of his choice, the prefect of the city, Priscus Attalus. Then, when he failed to get control of Honorius' provinces and found it impossible to get rid of Honorius, who had obtained help from the East, Alaric again marched on Rome (410) and this time did not stop to negotiate for a ransom but occupied the city and sacked it.

• *The Fall of Rome: The Reactions, West and East* The Roman world was horrified. Rome was "The *Urbs*," "The City," sacred and eternal, the symbol of Roman civilization. It had not been taken by a foreign enemy since the historic sack by the Gauls *ca.* 390 B.C. It had always been Rome's mission to subdue the barbarians and to introduce civilization among the non-Roman peoples; if barbarians now captured and plundered the ancient capital, it seemed that Roman civilization had come to an end. The end of Roman civilization was tantamount to the end of the world.

Pagans and Christians alike, for different reasons, regarded the catastrophe as a divine judgment. The excitement throughout the western provinces is reflected in the great work of St. Augustine, *De civitate Dei contra paganos,* "On the City of God, against the Pagans." St. Augustine wrote this vast work at intervals over a period of twenty years, as a refutation of pagan claims that the fall of the city was a well-merited manifestation of the Roman gods, angered by the desertion of Romans who had turned to a false Christian god. It had long been customary for pagans to explain public disasters by the intrusion of Christian falsehood. St. Augustine set out to show that the catastrophe was the inescapable result of the manner of life and the history of the pagan Roman empire. The fate of Rome, St. Augustine maintained, illustrated the different ways of life of the two communities that existed side by side in the Roman world, the City of Man and the City of God; the catastrophe demonstrated the inevitable consequences of these ways of life. In writing of a City of Man and a City of God, St. Augustine was employing the word *civitas* to denote any political organism, whether city, community, or state. The City of God was the whole Christian community leading a purposeful existence, just as the City of Man was the whole pagan community living according to its own desires.

As he contemplated the records of the "two cities," St. Augustine saw the lesson that to him illuminated the whole history of mankind, namely that a community or nation existed and possessed its identity on the basis of what its people loved. One could not understand the community, St. Augustine wrote, unless one understood this. In his *Politics*

Aristotle, developing the classic analysis of life in the Greek city, had been primarily concerned to determine and define the true purpose of life in a community. St. Augustine was not consciously following Aristotle's analysis, but he likewise saw the human community as the product of the real aims of its people.

St. Augustine's task was to study and compare two types of communities which differed fundamentally. The history of the pagan Roman state, to St. Augustine, was a history of lust of domination; its people wanted power, wealth, and the selfish enjoyment of earthly goods. It was a history of pomp and vanity in which men fought one another for material gain. The Christian community, founded on love and humbly seeking the glory of God, was the direct opposite. The City of Man, because of its nature, could come to only one end, exemplified by the catastrophe of Rome, while the City of God has its destined end in the consummation of the kingdom of God.

St. Augustine, with a thorough knowledge of the history and literature of Rome, recognized and paid tribute to the traditional virtues of the ancient Romans, which had brought their earthly empire to greatness; but this greatness, to St. Augustine, was not really what the Romans themselves believed it to be. In reality—and this was what the Romans were not able to understand—their pacification of the world had been a preparation for the coming of Christianity. For the time being, the City of Man and the City of God had to live together on earth, inextricably mingled physically but distinct in will. The City of Man would pass away while the City of God would endure. The Christian community was a true community; the pagan community was a false community.

As a statement of the Christian view of the nature of the historical process, St. Augustine's treatise has held a place of unique importance in historiography, just as the pagan interpretation of events can be seen in the pagan claims that St. Augustine and other Christian thinkers refuted. The

Christ as teacher, surrounded by the Apostles. Ivory box, now in the Staatliche Museen, Berlin. (*Hirmer Verlag, Munich*)

Christian historian saw the events of history, under the control of God, as the record of the salvation of mankind, moving toward an end which was foreordained, while the pagan chronicler looked forward to a future in which the events of history, following as it were a straight line, continued indefinitely taking place under the same powers (the gods, Fate, Chance, Fortune) that had governed men in the recorded past. Significantly of what Christian thinkers would have regarded as the pagans' fundamental ignorance of the truth, classical historians were not able to agree on the causes of events or on the nature of the powers that governed events; but whether the record of humanity was a series of cycles or a progression or regression of ages, or a mechanical sequence of cause and effect, the classical observer did not foresee the kind of consummation of the history of all mankind that the Christian scholar believed in.

The massive erudition and profound thought of St. Augustine's great book—not to speak of its literary mastery—establish it as the definitive treatment of the fall of Rome, illuminating the end of classical civilization and the beginning of the Middle Ages. Whether or not the sack of Rome was the final blow, Roman power in the West never recovered permanently. Within the century barbarian kings ruled the whole of the western provinces.

But modern readers of *The City of God* are not always aware that the fall of Rome did not make the same impression on the thought of the citizens in the East that it did in the West. Naturally the significance of the catastrophe itself was felt in the East, but no scholar or churchman there ever wrote a similar treatise on the Two Cities. Such a treatise was in fact unnecessary in the East. The reasons for this will be reviewed when the whole histories of East and West in the Late Empire have been examined. What is significant at this point is that St. Augustine's book in both conception and execution is a monument of Latin Christian thought, concerned entirely—as was natural—with the fate of Latin Rome.

In the East, the fall of Rome did not have the same meaning that the sack of Constantinople by German barbarians would have had. The capture of Rome did not, for the East, raise a question of the future of the empire and of the future of civilization. Both a City of Man and a City of God had existed in the East, but the terms of their existence had not been called into question by a public catastrophe. The East was physically secure; it was after the barbarians had failed in attempts on the eastern provinces that they had turned to Rome, whose military resources were weaker.

The absence of an eastern *City of God* exemplifies the extent of the separation that had grown up between the two halves of the empire. The government in Constantinople was able to send help on occasion to the government in Rome, but a centralized rule of East and West, with adequate military security of both at the same time, had now become impossible.

• *The End of Roman Rule in the West: The German Kingdoms* The remainder of Roman rule in the West is a confused and depressing story of the growing weakness of a government ruled precariously by a succession of emperors, ineffective for the most part, many of them under the control of barbarian generals. There was occasional assistance from Constantinople, but within the century even the nominal rule of an emperor in the West came to an end and the western provinces were turned into German kingdoms.

It is not possible here to trace all the complicated details of the anarchy in the West of which the sack of Rome was only the best-known episode and essentially the earliest. The economic and political conditions in the West were different from those in the East. Both halves of the empire were burdened by some of the same problems. The laws of the Code of Theodosius, published in East and West by order of Theodosius II in 438, show that the empire as a whole was suffering from difficulties that had long been familiar. The problems of agriculture and the scarcity of labor; industry which was not organized for adequate production; slow and expensive transportation; chronic financial difficulties of the municipalities and of the middle class; an elaborate and expensive civil service, many of whose officials were notoriously corrupt; high taxation for the upkeep of the civil service and the army—all these factors, for which no effective remedies could be found, tended to weaken both halves of the empire. Inevitably extremes of poverty and wealth persisted, while the trade in luxury goods gave no help to other economic problems. The upper classes were still cut off from the common people, still preoccupied with their own interests.

While these conditions were more or less common to East and West, the East, in compensation, enjoyed some advantages that the West lacked. Its resources in money, agriculture, and population were larger, and it was more stable politically. There had been fewer civil wars in the East than in the West, and correspondingly less waste of men and money.

The structure of the government differed significantly in East and West. In the West, the land-owning aristocrats, some of them fantastically wealthy, controlled the central administration, performing their duties with glaring inefficiency, favoring their own class, and contributing much less money than they should to the cost of the army and the government. The eastern empire, in contrast, possessed a civil service composed largely of middle-class professionals, and while graft unavoidably existed, the eastern government received in taxes a higher proportion of the national income than the western government could enjoy.

The greatest difference in the histories of the two halves of the empire was the result of geography. The West had to guard much longer frontiers—Rhine and upper Danube—while the East was threatened with barbarian invasion only across the lower Danube; and the East did not have to carry on war against Persia while the barbarians were invading the West.

This was the setting for the barbarian incursions that

plagued the western empire. The losses that the western army had suffered in Stilicho's time could not be made up. With the barbarians occupying the other provinces, recruiting had to be limited to Italy, and the Roman administration increasingly had to depend on hired barbarian troops. Often the Romans in the West would have to deal simultaneously with different barbarian tribes in different areas, and the Romans in the provinces, such as Britain, knowing that the government could send them no help, sometimes had to arm themselves and deal with the invaders as best they could.

About the time that Alaric sacked Rome, a large body of Burgundians crossed the Rhine and established themselves in Gaul. The Visigoths and Vandals, who had been living in Italy and Gaul, moved into Spain and in 429 the Vandals crossed into North Africa; the Roman authorities there could only recognize the accomplished fact.

A new threat appeared when the Huns, led by Attila, ravaged Thrace and Illyricum and invaded Italy in 452. When Attila died in the following year, the Huns broke up into small groups.

The assassination in 455 of the western emperor Valentinian III, the last surviving grandson of Theodosius I, opened a period of anarchy which ended twenty years later in the disappearance of Roman rule in the West. Gaiseric, the king of the Vandals in Africa, took advantage of the confusion that followed Valentinian's death and in the same year organized an invading army that entered Rome without resistance and for two weeks conducted a systematic sack of the city. The loot was fabulous. Some of it was recovered in 533 when Justinian's army destroyed the Vandal kingdom. The description by Procopius, Justinian's historian, of the recovered treasure carried in triumphal procession in Constantinople gives a vivid picture of the wealth that still existed in Rome while the barbarians were overrunning the West.

There had been a sharp reaction against German officers

after the debacle of Stilicho's career in 408, and although German names continued to be prominent in the army, Roman generals once more began to reach leading positions. The death of Valentinian III opened a new epoch of domination by German generals, experienced in Roman service, who were not qualified to become emperor themselves because of their foreign birth and because they were Arians—the barbarian nations were originally converted by Arian missionaries—but were able to place puppets on the throne. In the existing conditions, the puppets did not usually last long.

The most powerful of these barbarian officers was Ricimer, who was the dominant force in the western government for fifteen years. One of the emperors of this period, an experienced Roman army officer, Majorian, who was a protégé of Ricimer, proved to be an able ruler (457–461). He attempted to eliminate the administrative abuses that infested the western government and succeeded in reestablishing Roman authority in some of the provinces. But his energy was more than Ricimer considered suitable in an obedient protégé, and when an opportunity occurred, the emperor was taken into custody and executed by his patron.

When appointment to the imperial office depended on the favor of a barbarian officer, tenure could only be precarious. The principle of the collegiality of the western and eastern emperors became a fiction; unity of policy and action could scarcely be maintained. In the absence of collaboration with Constantinople, the Roman Senate was able to keep up some of the forms of traditional government, though it was now powerless to choose the emperors. There was a remnant of an aristocracy in the West and in Rome. Some extremely wealthy senators, owners of vast estates, were so influential, however, that they could not be compelled to give the government in Rome the financial help it badly needed. The rich senators managed to maintain possession of their properties during the entire period when Roman power was declining in the West.

Majorian had enjoyed the form of being proclaimed by the troops and elected emperor by the Senate in Rome, but he was never recognized by the eastern emperor, Leo I (457–474). Majorian's successor Severus (461–465) likewise was not granted recognition by Constantinople; however, when another change came, the emperor Leo was able to dictate the choice as the price of naval support from Constantinople for a projected expedition against the Vandals.

Leo's choice, the distinguished senator Anthemius (467–472), proved again to be too eminent a person for Ricimer to tolerate; the two came at last to open warfare and Anthemius was killed. Ricimer put an aristocrat, Olybrius, on the throne, but when both died soon after, command of the army passed to Ricimer's nephew Gundobad. After two more Romans occupied the throne briefly, Roman rule came to an end with the short reign (475–476) of a youth whose name, Romulus Augustulus, gave a pathetic touch to the end of the line of emperors in the West.

There was no further attempt to create a western emperor. Instead, Odoacer, the barbarian general who overthrew Romulus, endeavored to have himself recognized as the chief civil administrator of the West under the eastern emperor, Zeno (474–491). Zeno refused this recognition but was not in a position to insist on the election of a legitimate emperor. Odoacer was content to call himself king (*rex*), which was not a Roman imperial title.

In this fashion the Late Roman Empire in the West was succeeded by a group of barbarian kingdoms, the Burgundians in southeastern Gaul, the Visigoths in southwestern Gaul and Spain, the Vandals in Africa, the Franks in northern Gaul, the Ostrogoths in Italy. The contemporary sources indicate that the Roman population was surprisingly apathetic in the face of this upheaval. As has been seen, there were instances in which local populations, knowing that they could expect no help from the central government, armed themselves to offer what resistance they could. But for the most part civilians seem to have offered little resistance. Many people, of course, were not economically in a position to flee. The upper classes, who were able to escape, sometimes did so, but they sometimes remained and established relations with the invaders. The apparent apathy of the Roman population as a whole is perhaps explained by the fact that in the past the armies had been able to defend the frontiers, and the provinces had never suffered wholesale invasion and occupation; the experience was new.

The sources indicate that the invaders sometimes actively desired to establish good relations with the Roman population and that many of them were anxious to imitate the amenities of Roman life. The German kings found it convenient to retain the structure of the Roman civil administration they found in the provinces they occupied. They employed Romans as civil functionaries, just as the Arabs, after their conquest of Syria and Egypt, and the Turks, after their conquest of Byzantium, employed Byzantine civil servants, sometimes in high positions.

For the preservation of law and order, the German rulers adapted Roman law and Roman courts for the administration of justice among their Roman subjects. Most of the German kings seem to have wished to treat their Roman subjects fairly. Theodoric the Ostrogoth, who was king of Italy for thirty-three years (493–526), was an able ruler who admired Roman ways and showed respect for the Roman nobility. Under him the Senate in Rome actually grew in influence. The condition of Roman culture at this time, and the role played by prominent Romans in the new barbarian world, are illustrated by an extensive collection of the official correspondence of the senator Cassiodorus, a man of wide learning and the master of a lush literary style, who served in high administrative posts under the Ostrogothic kings between 506 and 538. With Pope Agapetus, he planned a Christian university in Rome which was to have a new type of curriculum whose goal was to be theological learning. The plan was never realized and instead Cassiodorus founded a monastery to which he retired to spend his time in literary work.

Another figure typical of the time was the aristocratic philosopher Boethius (*ca.* 480–524), son of a consul, who had an honorable career as a public official under Theodoric. His literary activity was so diversified that there has been doubt whether he was a pagan or a Christian. He planned to translate into Latin all the works of Plato and Aristotle, and composed a treatise on music. As an interpreter of Greek thought in Latin terms, he was a worthy successor of Cicero. Barbarians might occupy Rome, but they could not destroy its intellectual life and literary tradition.

• *The Eastern Empire in the Fifth Century: Chalcedon and the Monophysite Problem*   While Roman power in the West was in ignominious decline, the history of the empire of Constantinople followed a different course. Aside from occasional raids by Huns and by the bellicose Isaurian mountaineers of southern Asia Minor, the eastern provinces did not suffer the devastation that the West had to endure. If barbarians did succeed in getting across the lower Danube, the impregnable defenses of Constantinople prevented them from crossing into Asia Minor. Partly as a result of freedom from invasion, partly because government finances were better managed in the East, the army could be more adequately maintained, and this in turn reduced the danger from the barbarians.

In the East, too, the principal ministers of the government seem to have been more able. While the western regime of Honorius (395–423) was dominated by the emperor's generals, the administration in the East under his brother Arcadius (395–408) and under Arcadius' son Theodosius II (408–450) was directed by civilian officials. In the time of Arcadius and Theodosius II there came into existence a hereditary aristocracy of civil administrators whose efficiency is attested by the more stable conditions in that part of the empire. There were also "new men" rising from humble origins to the higher levels of the government.

Theodosius II became emperor at the age of seven. There
ensued a long regency of his masterful older sister Pulcheria, who directed her brother's education and impressed
upon him her own enthusiastic piety. Even after Theodosius II came of age, Pulcheria continued to control the government until one of the palace eunuchs, Chrysaphius, succeeded in securing supreme influence. Theodosius' energies
were directed toward scholarship and religion rather than
statecraft. His reign, however, was notable for the founding
of the university of Constantinople (425) and the publication of the Theodosian Code (438), an event of major importance in the history of Roman law.

The emperor Constantius had established a public library at Constantinople, and there is some evidence that he
inaugurated a university at the same time. If a university
did exist from this time, it may not have become a major
institution, for little or nothing is heard of its activities.
Institutions of higher learning had long existed at Athens
and Alexandria, and these may have been sufficient for the
need. Theodosius' university had fifteen professors of the
Greek language and literature, thirteen professors of the
Latin language and literature, one professor of philosophy,
and two professors of jurisprudence. Evidently the teaching
of philosophy was to be left to the schools of Athens and
Alexandria. The ample provision for Latin indicates that a
principal purpose of the university was preparation of
young men for the law and the civil service; Latin was still
the language of law and government in the Greek-speaking
half of the empire, where it had to be learned as a foreign
language. Theology was studied in a school under the control of the Church.

The Code, as a collection of the laws then in force, met a
long-standing need. In Roman judicial practice there had
never been a systematic method of empire-wide recording of
laws and decisions; no one could be sure of knowing all the
law on a given point. In the time of Diocletian two codes
were compiled by private initiative, but as legislation con-

tinued to be issued, need for codification continued. Theodosius' code included a collection of the legislation concerning the Church beginning with the reign of Constantine.

Developments in the history of the Church in these years
were momentous for the future of church and empire alike.
The aspirations to ecclesiastical power of the various patri-
archal sees were by this time sufficiently well-developed to
establish spheres of influence that had decisive effects not
only on theological problems but on secular politics. The
leaders of the Church formed what was called a pentarchy,
or "rule of five," composed of the patriarchs of the five sees
that had been founded by apostles—Jerusalem, Antioch,
Alexandria, Rome, and Constantinople. Constantinople
was a late arrival as its claim to have been founded by an
apostle (Andrew) was not established until the latter part
of the fourth century, whereas the historic claims of the
other sees had long been established.

Rome claimed a special place of honor among the other
sees on the ground of its having been founded by Peter, to
whom Christ had said (Matt. 16:18) "Thou art Peter
(*Petrus*), and upon this rock (*petra*) I will build my
church." However, when Constantinople became the imperial capital, its patriarch inevitably became the emperor's
chief ecclesiastical adviser. Indeed, a special rank was as-
signed to this see by the Council of Constantinople of 381,
which decreed that the see of Constantinople was to have
primacy of honor second only to that of old Rome.

Herein lay a seed of future trouble. Not only Rome, but
Antioch and especially Alexandria, as older in dignity than
Constantinople, resented dictation from the prelates of the
capital. In addition to occupying a place of honor based on
its ancient title, Rome stood in a special position because it
was the only apostolic foundation in the western provinces.
For this reason, as well as because it was the episcopal see in
the ancient western capital, it represented a single authority over the churches in the western provinces, whereas the
churches of the eastern provinces came under the jurisdic-

tion of four different patriarchates. While Rome had no rival in the West, the four patriarchates in the East were potential rivals among themselves. The eastern patriarchs had been accustomed to acknowledge the historic prestige of the bishop of Rome by submitting theological disputes for his judgment; the next step was for the Roman see to claim administrative jurisdiction as well as doctrinal authority over the eastern sees.

Naturally the popes of Rome were alert to enhance the prestige of their see when the diplomatic situation in the East offered an opportunity. A further situation that tended to enlarge the power of the Roman bishops was the decline of Roman political power in the West. As the government in Rome lost authority, the popes became the recognized custodians of law and order in the West. For example, Pope Innocent I (401–407) conducted the negotiations on one of the occasions when Alaric threatened Rome.

Under Theodosius II, the attention of the Church in the East became sharply focused on the continuing problem of the definition of the divine and human natures of Christ. Although the Arian controversy had officially been settled for some years, theologians continued to debate the technical aspects of Christology as they sought the means of expressing in human speech the mystery of the God-man. The New Testament portrayed a Christ who was obviously divine and evidently human. In what manner were the divine and human elements present in him? The universally acceptable statement of this mystery had not yet been reached. A crisis arose over the teaching of Nestorius, patriarch of Constantinople (428–431). Nestorius followed the tradition of thought which had been developed by the theologians of Antioch, who taught that it was necessary to emphasize the humanity in the dual nature of the Savior.

To the theologians of Alexandria, militant in their belief that the nature of Christ was essentially divine, Nestorius' doctrine was heresy. The Alexandrian patriarch Cyril demanded that a council be called to examine and condemn this error. Summoned to meet at Ephesus (431), the council was never regularly convened because some of the bishops were unable to arrive on time. Without waiting for them, Cyril and Nestorius, with their respective followers, met separately and voted canons which they claimed were decrees of the council. The party of Nestorius deposed Cyril and the party of Cyril deposed Nestorius. Cyril was able through bribery and influence to obtain his own restoration, while Nestorius was condemned and confined in his old monastery near Antioch.

The controversy remained unsolved, and another crisis flared up. A learned theologian, Eutyches, carried the doctrine of Alexandria to its extreme by maintaining that Christ had only one nature, the divine, which had absorbed the human nature. Here was a new variety of heresy. A second council was summoned to meet at Ephesus (449). The new patriarch of Alexandria, Dioscorus, presided, with the support of the emperor, whose intervention made it obvious what the action of the council would be. Eutyches was declared orthodox, and the council went down in history as the Latrocinium, "the Robber Council."

The theology of Alexandria seemed established, but within a year the situation changed. Theodosius II was killed while hunting when his horse stumbled. The new emperor, Marcian (450–457), needed recognition in the West, and Pope Leo I (440–461), highly displeased by the results of the recent council, insisted on a new meeting, which the emperor was obliged to summon.

After careful preparation by the imperial administration, a council assembled at Chalcedon (451). The proceedings of the second Council of Ephesus were condemned and a new definition of the nature of Christ was formulated, reaffirming the theology of the councils of Nicaea (325) and Constantinople (381). The definition declared that in Christ there existed two natures in one person, these natures being "united unconfusedly, unchangeably, indivisibly, and inseparably."

The Emperor Marcian. Colossal bronze statue in Barletta, Italy.
(*Hirmer Verlag, Munich*)

Alexandrian theologians were not satisfied because to them the definition was tainted with the heresy of Nestorius. Clergy, monks, and laity in Egypt and Palestine reacted violently to what they considered the denial of the supreme significance of Christ's divine nature. From their insistence on the ascendancy of the divine element in the Savior they were called Monophysites, or adherents of the "one-nature" doctrine. The supporters of the Chalcedonian theology proclaimed their faith with equal vehemence because to them denial of the reality of Christ's human nature was the denial of the efficacy of the Incarnation and of Christ's redeeming work.

Affecting as it did fundamentals of belief in the work of the Savior, the Monophysite controversy stirred the passions of people of all classes. Eventually the theological question became a political problem as well. Clergy and people in Egypt united solidly behind their ecclesiastical leaders. Monophysitism became the national religion, and whenever the government in Constantinople attempted to install a Chalcedonian patriarch in Alexandria, he had to be escorted to the city by imperial troops and his residence had to be guarded by soldiers to protect him from bodily harm. The movement gained strength increasingly in Palestine and Syria. Clashes between Monophysites and Chalcedonians, or between Monophysites and government troops, in the streets of Alexandria and of Antioch often ended in bloodshed. Here was grave trouble for the future. Feeling continued to be so strong that the people of Egypt, Palestine, and Syria were so far alienated from the central government that the conquest of these provinces by the Persians and then the Arabs in the seventh century was made easier.

In the years following the reign of Marcian (450–457) the eastern empire passed through a period of troubles, though these were not as perilous as those which the western empire had been experiencing. Once more the government was dominated by German generals in the Roman service. The most prominent, Aspar, had brought Marcian, a retired army officer, to the throne. When Marcian died, Aspar nominated another officer who became Leo I (457–474). Leo was able to free himself from the control of Aspar, but he failed to deal successfully with the continuing problem of the Gothic allies who were out of control in Dacia and Macedonia. Aspar's place of influence was taken by an Isaurian officer named Tarasicodissa, who became the emperor's favorite and took the Greek name of Zeno. After Leo's death and that of his son Leo II (474), Zeno became emperor (474–491).

Zeno's career was far from tranquil. As a member of the uncivilized nation of Isaurian mountaineers, he was a barbarian outsider in the eyes of his subjects of Greek and Roman descent, and especially unacceptable to the aristocrats of Constantinople. As an interloper of barbarian origin, he had to assure his position by means of the military support of his compatriots in the army. He could hardly have avoided a series of plots and revolts. One of these, the rebellion of another Isaurian general named Illus, is of interest because the rebels made a special effort to enlist the support of the pagans who were still to be found, apparently in substantial numbers, in several regions of the empire.

By methods that were not always praiseworthy Zeno contrived to keep his throne for seventeen years. In addition to the troubles caused by the insecurity of his position, the empire suffered from financial difficulties inherited from the extravagant operations of Leo I; at the same time Zeno had to spend considerable sums of money to keep the Goths quiet.

Zeno attempted to heal the breach in the Church by issuing the *Henotikon*, or "decree of union," containing a fresh statement of faith that would, it was hoped, take the place of the disputed Chalcedonian definition. The formula, omitting reference to the problem of the number of natures in Christ, consisted chiefly of a restatement of the theology of the councils of Nicaea and Constantinople. It actually made important concessions to the Monophysites, but it was considered unacceptable both by the pope and by the extremist wing of the Egyptian Monophysites.

At Zeno's death an elderly civil servant, Anastasius, was chosen as his successor (491–518). Anastasius promptly broke the power of the Isaurians and brought about reforms of the administration and elimination of waste which enabled him to achieve the financial rehabilitation of the empire for which he is well known.

A man of strong religious feeling, Anastasius was a Monophysite in his personal beliefs. The patriarch of Constantinople agreed to play his role in the coronation only if the new emperor would give him a written statement that he would respect the pronouncements of the Council of Chalcedon—a condition that the emperor was bound to resent. In his first twenty years, Anastasius followed a neutral policy in the controversy, but when the strength of the Chalcedonians alarmed the emperor, he began (511) to support the Monophysites openly. Vitalian, commander of the barbarian troops in Thrace, raised a rebellion in the Chalcedonian cause but was eventually defeated by the imperial forces.

Thanks to frugalities and to the efficiency of the tax collectors, Anastasius restored the government to a sound footing financially. A major improvement was the introduction of a new method of calculating with some accuracy the amounts of the taxes that should be paid in goods and in money. Some of the most burdensome taxes were abolished or reduced; currency was reformed; considerable sums were spent on public works and on frontier fortifications; and it was possible to send large armies against the rebel Vitalian and against the Persians, who had opened hostilities in 502. At the same time the emperor managed to accumulate reserves in the treasury which at the time of his death amounted to the very considerable sum of 320,000 pounds of gold.

The literary history of Anastasius' reign offers a pleasant glimpse of the literary culture that had flourished in the Greek East since Hellenistic times. Athens and Alexandria continued to be celebrated for their communities of scholars. The little city of Gaza had become a famous center for advanced studies in Greek literature and philosophy, which began a notable period of prosperity in the time of Anastasius. Work centered around a distinguished group of teachers, many of them trained at Alexandria. Every year the city held a festival which was a combination of fair and literary symposium, and visitors from all over the empire came to enjoy the fair and to hear the professors read their own works in the theater. Gaza itself, with fine temples, colonnades, and gardens, and a climate famous for its mildness, provided the setting of a classical Greek *polis*. The annual festival was considered so important that the expense was subsidized by the government.

The activity of the schools at Gaza, which continued to flourish in the reign of Justinian, exemplified the new scholarship of the Christian professors who wrote on both theological and classical themes. The writings of the classical Greek historians and philosophers formed the core of the curriculum, and students from all over the Greek East, including the future historian Procopius, came to Gaza for the final stages of their literary training. The same professors who supervised classical studies wrote treatises on theology and Biblical exegesis.

The death of Anastasius was followed by the brief reign (518–527) of a compromise candidate, Justin, commander of the palace guard. He brought the eastern empire to the opening of the brilliant epoch of his nephew Justinian the Great (527–565), which marks the transition of the Late Roman Empire to the Byzantine Empire. The western provinces had now for some years been parceled into German kingdoms, while Theodoric the Ostrogoth ruled as king in Italy. At this point, therefore, it is appropriate to review the explanations that have been offered to account for the decline of Roman power in the West, and at the same time to recall the reasons why the same kind of decline did not take place in the East as well.

• *"Decline and Fall": The Problem for Modern Scholarship*   The decline and fall of the ancient world have been one of the most fascinating, and in some ways one of the most baffling, problems that modern historians have been called upon to study. "Decline" and "fall" are actually two different things, which must be studied separately. Scholars today are no longer sure, as Gibbon was, that there was a decline and fall in the terms of the massive process he depicted. Rather the modern student sees the process as transformation, aptly described for example by the French historian Ferdinand Lot in the English form of the title he chose for his book, *The End of the Ancient World and the Beginnings of the Middle Ages.*

In endeavoring to explain the collapse of a state once so powerful as the Roman Empire, scholars have brought to bear all the resources of modern critical research, but the varied character of some of the explanations that have been offered only emphasizes the intricacy of the problem, complicated as it is by the loss of important evidence such as is available for the study of similar problems in more recent times. Repeated efforts have been made to isolate one cause and make it basically responsible, as specialists have proposed to trace the decline, for example, to the barbarian invasions, or to soil exhaustion, or to lack of manpower, or to corruption in the bureaucracy, or to dilution of Roman blood by the admixture of inferior strains, or to the gradual extermination of the aristocratic leadership, or to a change in climate (a theory, once popular, that is not supported by any sure evidence).

It may seem that explanations of this kind deal with symptoms rather than with efficient causes. It seems plain that the economy of the empire was not adequate to the demands for defense purposes that were made upon it.

For one of the most important problems, the question whether there was a real decline in population, no really satisfactory evidence exists.

In any case the variety of the explanations of the decline that have been offered suggest an important consideration, namely that a variety of interrelated factors can be seen at work which, as A. H. M. Jones, one of the most distinguished students of the problem, has pointed out, scholars will attempt to disentangle at their peril.

Jones has also emphasized another consideration of major importance which has not always been taken into account. This is (as has been noted) that some of the conditions that have been identified as causes of decline existed in both the eastern and western divisions of the empire, but while the western power collapsed in the latter part of the fifth century, the eastern empire preserved its independence for another thousand years, until the fall of Constantinople in 1453. The scholars who have written on the decline have for the most part been historians of the West who have not taken sufficiently into consideration the different experience of the eastern empire at the time of the decline of the West, such as it has been described earlier in this chapter. The eastern empire had a better chance to survive, and was better prepared to do so.

The following chapter will trace the history of the East, so different from that of the West, during the reign of Justinian, the brilliant epoch that in itself serves as a commentary on the decline of the West.

5 The Empire of Constantinople

• *Justinian, "the Emperor Who Never Slept"* Justinian's long (527–565) and eventful reign constituted an epoch that scholars have taken as the point at which all the threads of the history of the Late Roman Empire came together. His historian Procopius has left a striking picture of an energetic and conscientious ruler, more active and more ambitious than many of his predecessors, who regularly worked far into the night; people commonly remarked that he never slept.

Not the least of Justinian's resources was the intelligence and talent of his consort Theodora. Procopius' libelous description of her personality has overshadowed the real importance of her contribution to her husband's career. After her death from cancer in 548, when Justinian was in his middle sixties, there was a marked change in the emperor's personality.

Justinian was a well-read student of history and his program was a renewal of the Roman Empire in all its aspects. Territory lost to the barbarians was to be recovered and the Mediterranean was to become once more "Our Sea" (*mare nostrum*), in the phrase made famous by Julius Caesar. The laws and the courts were to be reformed; the imperial administration was to be overhauled; the provinces were to be reorganized and freed from administrative abuses; and an extensive building program was to be inaugurated throughout the empire.

One of Justinian's most valuable gifts was the ability to discover and inspire subordinates who possessed notable talents in many fields. One result is that today Justinian's reign is known through a number of tangible monuments— the codification of the law carried out by Tribonian; the Church of St. Sophia at Constantinople designed by Anthemius and Isidorus; the church of the monastery of St. Catherine on Mount Sinai; the literary work of Procopius, Paul the Silentiary, Agapetus, Agathias, and the poets of the day whose work is preserved in the *Greek Anthology*; and the remains of public buildings in all parts of his empire. Mosaics, medallions, jewelry, and silverware preserved in museums illustrate the magnificence of this reign in which the distinctive civilization of Byzantium is to be seen emerging.

• *Ruler and Subjects* When Justinian became sole emperor, he had already had the advantage of an apprenticeship during the reign of his elderly uncle Justin I (518–527), during which Justinian had been the power behind the throne. This period of observation gave Justinian an opportunity to study the problems of the empire and to plan the programs which he put into effect soon after his accession.

Justinian became emperor without difficulty when his uncle co-opted him as Augustus during his last illness. The new emperor began his reign with the energy that characterized his whole career; but his policies had to be carried out under the immediate scrutiny of the two classes of his subjects with which he was in immediate contact in Constantinople, the senatorial nobility and the common people.

The senatorial nobility of Constantinople was not as old or as wealthy as that of old Rome had been. It was a mixed group. Some of its members belonged by right of inheritance; others had been elevated from lower rank and appointed by the emperor. Nevertheless it was an influential body with vast holdings of landed property and an accumulation of wealth which was carefully kept within the order by means of judicious marriages. Not all the members of the order took an active part in government, though a strong tradition of public service had developed in some families. Many preferred to live at leisure in their elegant country villas in the provinces, and visited their palaces in Constantinople only when necessary. Though their pedigrees were not always long and their role in the Senate itself was now largely perfunctory, the members of the order were highly class conscious, proud of their breeding and culture, and concerned for the elaborate titles of rank by which they were carefully arranged in order of precedence at court and in the administration.

While Justinian had been appointed to senatorial rank during his uncle's reign, many of the aristocrats in the capital looked upon him as an outsider. Justin had been a peasant—malicious gossip said that he was illiterate, which could hardly have been true. When he became emperor, Justinian's detractors poked fun (discreetly, of course) at his provincial accent in speaking Greek, which was looked upon as a blemish reflecting his rustic origin in a region where Latin alone was in use. Elegant society in Constantinople spoke Greek.

Moreover, Justinian's inheritance of his office was a reminder to the senatorial nobility of the circumstances in which his uncle had become emperor. Anastasius had left no designated heirs, but he had three nephews, Hypatius, Probus, and Pompeius, any one of whom might have seemed a natural choice to succeed him. There were several other candidates put forward by various groups, and after a good bit of indecision Justin was chosen by the Senate. Ostensibly he was selected because he was elderly (in the middle sixties) and was supposed to be acceptable to all parties. Actually there was some reason to believe that Justin was not a compromise candidate chosen because other factions could not put their candidates on the throne, but that his election was really the result of a carefully planned intrigue. In any case, this history meant that Justinian

Gold medallion of Justinian. (*Crown Copyright, British Museum*)

would not be able to count upon the wholehearted support of the senatorial nobility.

The other group of his subjects with which the emperor was in immediate contact was the city mob of Constantinople. Like all the city mobs in the empire, this one was composed of idlers who drew free rations of bread and were provided with free entertainments in the hippodrome, where the chariot races, which were the main spectacles, were interspersed with shows of jugglers, acrobats, trained bears, and other similar performances, some of which were of a less edifying character.

In Constantinople and in other major cities the common people were organized in two circus factions, the Blues and the Greens, whose members were partisans of the two stables that competed in the chariot races. The leading charioteers, who wore the colors of their stables, were popular heroes, and their cheering supporters sat on opposite sides of the hippodrome, shouting insults at each other.

The Blues and Greens of Constantinople, from being sporting factions, had developed a degree of solidarity as forces for the expression of popular feeling which the government was compelled to recognize. While they had no legal standing as political parties, they expressed their opinions freely, and were permitted to address the emperor in the hippodrome through heralds.

The factionists in the capital were well aware of their influence and showed their independence by defying customs of dress, leaving hair and beard uncut and wearing outlandish garments in barbarian style. Assembled in the hippodrome, they made a bizarre spectacle, but they were a political force that not many years after Justinian became emperor caused a crisis of the most serious magnitude, known as the "Nika riots" of January 532. These riots actually amounted to a rebellion.

What began as an ordinary brawl between supporters of rival charioteers, such as was not uncommon in the hippodromes of Constantinople and other cities, grew into a major riot in which, after the initial outbreak had been suppressed by the city authorities, the two factions joined forces and demanded that Justinian dismiss three of his ministers who had made themselves unpopular by the rigorous fashion in which they were performing their duties. On successive days the disorders spread through the city as the rioters burned and pillaged, crying their Greek watchword *nika!* (win!). The old Church of St. Sophia, built by Constantine and Constantius, was burned.

The emperor, displaying a surprising lack of courage, agreed to dismiss the unpopular officials, but the rioting from being an outbreak provoked by popular grievances now turned into an attempt to overthrow the emperor and involved not only the common people but the aristocracy and the relatives of the emperor Anastasius who had been candidates to succeed him but had lost to Justin I. How much of the original rioting had been encouraged by discontented aristocrats cannot be determined, but these certainly took advantage of the disorders. The rioting became rebellion when the mob proclaimed as emperor Anastasius' nephew Hypatius, who had the support of a number of senators who thought there was a chance of getting rid of Justinian.

The emperor, who must have had some idea of the existence of opposition to his policies but may not have realized its extent, was so alarmed that he prepared to flee. Theodora, learning of her husband's plan, intervened dramatically and rebuked the emperor and his advisers for their cowardice. Belisarius, who was present, probably was the source for Procopius' account of the empress' words: "May I never exist without this purple robe and may I never live to see the day on which those who meet me shall not address me as 'Your Majesty.' If you wish, O Emperor, to save yourself, there is no difficulty; we have ample funds. Yonder is the sea, and there are the ships. Yet reflect whether, when you have once escaped to a place of security, you will not prefer death to safety. *I* agree with an old saying that 'Empire is a fair winding-sheet.' "

Belisarius and his colleague Mundus, who was also in the

palace at the time, undertook to attack the rebels with
troops that the two generals had with them. Belisarius and
Mundus secretly led their men into the hippodrome and
began a battle with the factionists that turned into a massacre. It is recorded that thirty thousand people were killed.
Hypatius and his brother Pompeius were executed the next
day. The senators who had supported Hypatius were exiled
and their property was confiscated. Justinian could have
been much more severe at the time. Later he allowed the
exiled senators to return and restored their property to
them; he also gave the property of Hypatius and his brother
to their sons.

The suppression of the riots left Justinian stronger than
before. But the strength displayed by the rioters showed
how precarious the basis of the monarchy might be, and the
brutal force used to suppress the disorders showed that the
political theory which pictured a benevolent ruler chosen
and guided by God had to be supplemented by practical
measures.

• *Sacerdotium and Imperium*   Having demonstrated in
the suppression of the Nika rebellion that his rule could be
maintained by force in traditional style, Justinian proclaimed a carefully phrased statement of his conception of
the ideological basis of the power of the imperial office and
its role in the administrative structure of the Christian
Roman state. In this statement Justinian defined in his own
terms the relationship between the sovereign and the
Church, a subject that had presented problems to emperors
and churchmen since the days of Constantine. It had only
been possible to make the concept of a state church an
administrative reality in the time of Theodosius I. Justinian, always conscious that he was God's chosen vice-gerent,
proceeded to formulate his own statement of the nature of
the state that he ruled.

This pronouncement was embodied in *Novella* VI, a law
issued in 535. In the preface the emperor declares that the

greatest of the divine gifts to mankind are (in the order mentioned) the priestly office (*sacerdotium*) and the imperial office (*imperium*). The former ministers to mankind in spiritual matters, the latter presides over human affairs, but both come from the same divine origin. It is the responsibility of the Roman emperors to care for the honorable estate of the priesthood, because the well-being of the state depends on the well-being of the priestly order and the correctness of the belief concerning God that is held by everyone in the state. Hence, the emperor declares, he has the greatest solicitude for orthodox belief and for the proper condition of the *sacerdotium*, for it is in this way that the greatest gifts of God have been given to the state and will be given in the future.

Justinian's concept of the imperial office was not new but the statement of the relationship of *sacerdotium* and *imperium* was his own. He is careful to speak of two powers within the state, *sacerdotium* and *imperium*; he does not speak in terms of individuals, the priests (*sacerdotes*) and the emperor (*imperator*) who fill these offices and use these powers. The Christian Roman state is defined as a single body consisting of two parts, which today would be called the ecclesiastical and the political, each with its responsibility for a particular sphere of human life. Each part contributes to the other, and the nature of the emperor's office is such that he is responsible for good order and harmony in both parts. This responsibility of the emperor's is of divine origin; Justinian does not claim that it comes to him from the earthly *sacerdotium*.

The word order, *sacerdotium*, then *imperium*, is significant, not only because it indicates Justinian's ranking of their importance, but because it suggests that there was present here the Old Testament conception of the king as the chief person, from a religious point of view, as exemplified in Saul, David, and Solomon.

In other laws Justinian emphasized that all his activity as ruler stemmed from and was guided by his love toward his

subjects (*philanthropia*), which was one of the most important of the traditional virtues of the ideal Roman ruler.
Nevertheless he did not hesitate to speak of his people as his
"subjects." Previous emperors in their laws had referred to
their people as "citizens" or "Roman citizens." Justinian's
usage might sound autocratic, but it was in fact a recognition of an existing situation.

• *The Emperor and the Law*   Defects in many branches
of the administration of the law had accumulated during
the Late Roman Empire, and Justinian worked to remove
these difficulties, which bore hard on his subjects, especially
the poorer ones, when they needed to go to law.

To begin with, the laws themselves were not readily accessible because of the unsystematic way in which they were
published. By Justinian's time the existing collections of
laws, the privately compiled Gregorian and Hermogenian
codes, dating from the reign of Diocletian, and the Theodosian Code of 438, had become obsolete because of the mass
of legislation and commentary that had appeared after
these collections were compiled. Having been in a position
to observe the situation during the reign of his uncle Justin
I, Justinian was convinced that one of the greatest needs of
the empire was a thorough revision of the whole law. Six
months after he became sole emperor he appointed a com-
mission of distinguished legal experts who were directed to
examine all the existing laws, eliminate obsolete and con-
tradictory material, abbreviate where necessary, and orga-
nize in a usable form what was valid.

The resulting *Corpus Iuris Civilis*, comprising the *Code*
(534), the *Digests*, and the *Institutes* (533, an official text-
book for students), supplemented by the *Novellae*, or "new
laws," which were issued after publication of the Code, was
one of the great monuments of Justinian's reign. Due credit
should go of course to the committee of learned jurists
headed by Tribonian, who carried out their task under the
emperor's inspiration.

The arrangement of the Code is typical of the way in which the organization of the laws had been brought up to date. Laws pertaining to the Church and civil laws were now introduced in the same compilation and under the same headings; in the compilation of Theodosius II, laws pertaining to ecclesiastical matters had been collected in a final division (Book XVI) following the main body of the material, which was arranged in the traditional pre-Christian order.

At the beginning of the Code, Justinian stated that he regarded himself as bound to observe the laws: "Our authority depends on the authority of the law, and indeed the subordination of sovereignty under the law is a greater thing than the imperial power itself." The emperor likewise was careful to declare that God had sent him to mankind as the "living law" (*lex animata*), a principle of Hellenistic kingship that had been taken over into Roman political theory, though the principle had also been established, in the early third century A.D., that the emperor must consider himself bound to act in accordance with the laws.

The courts and the administration of justice were also badly in need of reform—how badly, the scope of Justinian's reforms indicates. In the Late Roman Empire the administration of justice had become slow and expensive for the litigants. Special courts had come into existence in unsystematic fashion, and there were conflicts of jurisdiction and of appeal everywhere. The supreme courts in Constantinople were burdened with minor litigation. In many instances judges were civil administrators rather than trained jurists, though some of them could have legal advisers.

Justinian instituted a plan—in effect a revival of a measure of the emperor Zeno's—to make available judges who were learned in the law. Conflicting jurisdictions were eliminated wherever possible, and the system of appeals was put in better order. Laws were passed limiting the time during which prisoners might be kept in custody awaiting trial, and generous arrangements for bail were made. Bishops received instructions to see that the governors of prisons kept the rules; the bishops themselves were ordered to visit the prisons weekly to talk with the prisoners.

• *The Tasks of Imperium* Other reforms were badly needed in the vast and complicated administrative machinery. Justinian himself had a detailed practical knowledge of the working of the bureaucracy, and he showed a real interest in relieving the people of the provinces of many of the abuses from which they suffered as a result of the corruption of local officials.

Many of the reforms were probably devised by the able minister John the Cappadocian. The administration of the provinces was simplified in the interests of efficiency and economy. Before Justinian's time, in fact as early as the time of Constantine, cabinet officers in Constantinople had in effect sold governorships of provinces, and the governors when in office had to reimburse their expenses by extortion. Justinian put a stop to this and endeavored to find better men as governors. Other measures for the relief of the provincials were aimed at more efficient collection of the revenue and improvement in the administration of justice on the local level.

One of Justinian's best-known activities was his building program. There seems to have been need for construction of all kinds in all parts of the empire, including improvement of fortifications on the borders. Some large cities, such as Antioch and some cities in North Africa, had shrunk in size and needed to have their fortifications contracted to save manpower. Procopius recorded an empire-wide program of construction of a magnificence that recalled the lavish expenditure of the emperors of the greatest days of the empire. This work provided the emperor with an appropriate occasion for display of munificence. He renamed his birthplace in Illyricum Justiniana Prima (modern Scupi), and gave his name to at least a dozen other cities.

Hospitals, orphanages, homes for old people, and hostels for travelers were built in Constantinople and the provinces. Hospitals for pilgrims were endowed in Palestine. In the capital, the splendid Church of St. Sophia was only one of a number of fine churches; the emperor himself took part in drawing the plans. Procopius' account indicates that there was a well-balanced plan for the improvement of Constantinople, which incidentally provided work for the unemployed. Public buildings, harbors, parks, a new entrance to the palace, and a bronze equestrian statue of the emperor on a pillar in the main square of the city, all helped to make Constantinople one of the most beautiful cities of the world.

Justinian was not content to rule the empire in the state to which it had been reduced by the barbarian conquests in the West. Historically, the empire could not be the empire without the lost territories. At the same time, it had been a historic task of Rome to keep in check the power of Persia. The Persian state, unlike the other barbarian nations on the fringes of the empire, had a stable regime and an organized army. Thus an ambitious Persian monarch could create a continuing military problem for the Romans. Given the need to prepare costly expeditions for the reconquest of North Africa from the Vandals and of Italy and Spain from the Ostrogoths, Justinian at the same time had to wage with Persia the war he had inherited from Anastasius and Justin I.

The plan for the invasion of North Africa was opposed by the emperor's advisers, who considered the available resources insufficient. However, under the generalship of Belisarius, the campaign was successful (533–534), and the treasure of the Vandal kings that had been looted from the Romans brought timely assistance to the imperial treasury.

The campaign in Italy, which Justinian launched as soon as possible (535), proved a much more difficult undertaking. The Persians broke a treaty of peace in 540 and succeeded in capturing and burning Antioch. Justinian found himself with major wars on two widely separated fronts, plus operations against the Moors, who were raiding the recently conquered territory in North Africa. Though money seems to have been available, Justinian appears to have been unwilling to allow the commanders in Italy sufficient resources to complete the reconquest promptly. The resulting prolongation of the fighting until 561 brought devastation from which the peninsula was long in recovering. Only a part of Spain could be reoccupied temporarily (550–554), while there were regular raids into Thrace by Sclavenes, Bulgars, and other tribes.

One of the miracles of Justinian's reign seems to have been that in general the budget was balanced, thanks to the financial skill of his ministers John the Cappadocian and Peter Barsymes, and to the efficiency of the tax collectors. Peter Barsymes instituted the famous state monopoly in silk fabrics, which brought handsome profits. Justinian at the beginning of his reign was able to draw on the surplus in the treasury left by Anastasius, and the treasure of the Vandal kings helped pay for the building of St. Sophia. In general, however, expenses seem to have been met from revenue. In Justinian's last years, when his powers were failing, money seems to have been wasted and the army was allowed to shrink dangerously for lack of funds. Justinian's successor, his nephew Justin II, complained about his uncle's wasteful policies, but he seems to have been able to make up for the shortages in the treasury without undue difficulty. Justinian's real failure here seems to have been that he could not find the means to maintain an army large enough to secure the empire that he had re-established.

• *The Problems of Sacerdotium* The imbroglio of the Monophysite controversy that Justinian inherited had before his time grown to be far more than a dispute among theologians over the definition of the union of the divine and human natures of Christ. The controversy not only produced massive public disorders in the provinces of Justinian's realm, but affected the religious and political relations of Constantinople with Rome and the Ostrogothic kingdom in Italy. A breach with Rome, whose pontiffs had stoutly maintained the Chalcedonian doctrine, had existed since the reign of Zeno, when Pope Felix III in 484 had excommunicated both the patriarch of Constantinople, Acacius, and the emperor himself because the emperor in an effort to reconcile the Chalcedonians and Monophysites had published a formula of union (the *Henotikon*). Rome objected that the emperor had no authority to issue a pronouncement on doctrine, a function which had always been considered to belong to the bishops in council.

Constantinople had had to accept the schism with Rome since the measures necessary to heal the breach would have caused further difficulties in the effort to reconcile the Monophysites. In the reign of Anastasius, who tolerated the Monophysites, peace with Rome would have been impossible; but as soon as Justin I succeeded Anastasius, reconciliation with Rome became a matter of prime importance in Constantinople, and in 519 the patriarch of the capital signed a reaffirmation of Chalcedonian doctrine that had been dispatched for his signature by Pope Hormisdas. The reconciliation was politically important not only for Constantinople but for King Theodoric in Italy.

In the eastern provinces the stubborn allegiance to the Monophysite theology in Syria and Egypt had begun to find expression in terms of cultural nationalism. The violent feelings in these ancient provinces, which looked upon the government in Constantinople as alien in race and language, as well as oppressive, created a political problem that in Justinian's time seemed to threaten the disruption of the empire. Attempts by the government to maintain a hierarchy of Chalcedonian prelates in Syria and Egypt continued to produce riots and bloodshed. The Monophysite leaders in Syria maintained a separate church, with its own hierarchy, who had to live in disguise and hold services in private. At one time Justinian even instituted a special campaign for the extermination of the Monophysites in Syria, who were systematically hunted down by troops, and, when found, were burned to death on the spot. The operation failed to bring the desired results and had to be abandoned.

Since the leaders of the Church had been unable to settle the Christological dispute in spite of repeated attempts over many years, the emperor, acting on the basis of his responsibility for the good order of the empire entrusted to him by God, determined to find a formula himself that would be acceptable to both parties, who by this time, as happens in such controversies, had stopped listening to each other. Justinian, a religious person by nature, and well versed in theology, was confident that he was equipped to find a solution.

Among the Monophysites there was a moderate party which might be more open to reconciliation. Justinian began by seeking a means of defining Christ's human nature that could be accepted by the less fanatical Monophysite theologians. There already existed such a formula, which would preserve the reality of the divine nature of Christ even though it was believed that in his human nature he suffered in the flesh on the cross. Hoping that this concept would be accepted by both Monophysites and Chalcedonians, Justinian on his own initiative promulgated a doctrine of the Church in the form of an imperial edict in 533. Since formulations of doctrine were supposed to be determined only by ecumenical councils, the emperor's action was a bold step, justified in his own eyes by the seriousness of the stalemate. The pope, John II, anxious to preserve harmony between Constantinople and Rome, gave his assent to the formula, but it was unacceptable to the rigid thinkers among both Monophysites and Chalcedonians.

Here Justinian found himself involved in far more than the theological problem. His plans for the reconquest of the West made it essential for him to seek the support of the

Justinian in procession to celebration of Holy Communion, escorted by bodyguard and preceded by bishop and priests. Mosaic in the Church of San Vitale, Ravenna. (*Anderson-Alinari*)

bishops in Italy, where sentiment was uniformly Chalcedonian. At the same time he had to take into account the
activities of Theodora, whose personal inclination toward
Monophysite belief led her to give secret assistance to
Monophysite leaders.

In time the emperor, still searching for a means of reconciliation, found another opening in the condemnation of
the teaching of certain theologians whose doctrine formed a
stumbling block for the Monophysites because their ideas
seemed tainted with heresy. Again Justinian took independent action and published the condemnation in an imperial edict (546). The eastern patriarchs were forced to
assent, but again the emperor had succeeded in provoking
the opposition of Rome. The pope, Vigilius, raised the
proper objection that only an ecumenical council could
promulgate a revision of doctrine. Vigilius was brought to
Constantinople—whether willingly or under duress is not
clear—in an effort to persuade him to agree to the imperial
pronouncement. In the capital, the pope was subjected to
pressure, including physical coercion, and wavered between
acceptance and rejection of the edict. Finally he gave his
assent (548), but three years later withdrew it.

Meanwhile opposition to the decree among the eastern
bishops grew and Justinian renewed the edict in 551. Finally the emperor consented to the summoning of an ecumenical council. The council met in 553, its members carefully chosen to assure approval of the imperial theology.
The bishops endorsed the emperor's action, and Pope Vigilius, still in Constantinople, could only accept their vote.

Once more, however, Justinian's attempt failed to reconcile the Monophysites, and the political problem in the
eastern provinces remained unsolved, while relations of
Constantinople with the western church had scarcely been
improved. But Justinian in his old age did not lose hope. In
his last years he found another formula that he believed
would serve as a basis for reconciliation, namely a proposal
to the effect that the human flesh that Christ possessed was
to be distinguished from ordinary human flesh.

Justinian did not take into account that the Monophysites had already rejected this proposal; nor had experience taught him that in a controversy where feeling was so strong, compromise, as such, had little chance of success. In 565, the last year of his life (he was about eighty-three years old), Justinian published his doctrine, again in the form of an edict. It brought violent opposition from both parties. Justinian was preparing to use force to have the edict accepted, but his death forestalled the disorders that would have followed.

• *"Caesaropapism"* In the history of the Church Justinian earned the name of a tyrant, and his assumption of the right to formulate doctrine was certainly beyond his recognized powers. However, an assessment of the emperor's theological activities must distinguish between the view accepted at that time of the responsibility of the emperor, and the methods Justinian employed in carrying out what he considered to be his responsibility. His unilateral formulation of doctrine was certainly an arrogation of a function that had always been understood to belong only to the bishops meeting in council under the guidance of the Holy Spirit; but this action was taken because he believed that this was the only way he could settle a controversy that was threatening the stability not only of the Church but of the state, for both of which he was responsible to God.

Justinian's interference in the spiritual affairs of the Church is cited as a classic example of what some scholars have called caesaropapism. In the modern understanding of caesaropapism as the supremacy of the civil power in the control of ecclesiastical affairs, Justinian's conduct does indeed constitute caesaropapism. Here however care must be taken in the use of the term. Caesaropapism is a word of modern invention, not found in the ancient writers. It is significant that none of the actions of the Byzantine rulers that have been described as instances of caesaropapism had a lasting effect on the Church. Indeed the Church was too old and too vast to suffer permanent alteration of doctrine at the hands of an earthly and transitory ruler. What has happened is that the concept of caesaropapism, which can indeed be found in the western church in the medieval era, has been erroneously transferred to the eastern church.

In Justinian's conception of the relation of the emperor to the Church, which was also the conception of his Byzantine successors, the imperial office and the Church were parallel and cooperative but not completely identical aspects of human society. As vice-gerent of God the emperor had a responsibility for the welfare of the Church as an institution and for the welfare of the Christian people. In the presence of the Monophysite problem Justinian was forced, he thought, to intervene in an impasse that threatened the unity of the empire. His effort failed because, as later experience showed, any settlement would have been impossible at that time; but his apprehension concerning the possible political consequences of the controversy was justified, for when the Persians and then the Arabs invaded Egypt, Palestine, and Syria in the seventh century, the people of those provinces, still Monophysites, looked upon the invaders as less oppressive masters than the hated government in Constantinople.

• *Athens, Jerusalem, Constantinople* One of the principal reasons why Justinian's reign formed an epoch was that the emperor had a vision of a synthesis of all aspects of life —political, religious, intellectual—that should complete the development of the Christian Greco-Roman society in what he conceived to be its true form. The working out of this synthesis had been in progress since the time of Constantine, but the task had been too great for Justinian's predecessors to complete in all details. Justinian considered that it was granted to him to bring this whole process to fulfillment.

Although Christianity had been the recognized national religion for two hundred years, a number of pagans, surviving in spite of sporadic persecution, continued to practice the ancient rites in secret. Since the empire could play its part in the Christian scheme of history only if all its members were adherents of the true faith, Justinian placed all dissenters on the same footing and inaugurated a program for the elimination of heretics, pagans, Jews, and Samaritans. In 529, soon after he became sole emperor, all pagans were commanded to receive Christian instruction and to be baptized. If they refused, they were to be exiled and their property was to be confiscated.

The order was only partly successful, and in 542, in a special campaign, seventy thousand pagans in the country regions of Asia Minor were forcibly baptized. In Constantinople a number of prominent persons were tried, convicted of pagan practices, and executed, though the great jurist Tribonian, perhaps on account of his eminence, was able to remain a pagan. When it proved impossible to convert all of them, heretics, pagans, Jews, and Samaritans were placed under civil disabilities and forbidden to hold public office or to teach.

The comprehensiveness of the measures by which dissidents were excluded from the Christian society recalls the terms in which the emperor Julian had envisioned the elimination of Christianity and the restoration of the classical empire. Julian forbade Christians to teach classical subjects, Justinian forbade all dissenters from orthodox Christianity to teach anything at all. But the problem of the intellectual framework of society was a different one for Justinian. For Julian, it would have been impossible to conceive of utilizing any aspect of Christian thought in the traditional classical educational program. On the contrary, by Justinian's time Christian intellectual leaders in both the eastern and western halves of the empire had long been glad to transform into Christian terms the best elements of classical moral training, philosophical thought, and literary craftsmanship.

This process had brought into being a new type of Christian professor, who taught the substance of the classical tradition from the point of view of the Christian faith. Flourishing schools conducted on these principles at Gaza and Alexandria provided advanced training in literature, rhetoric, and philosophy. A professor in these establishments would write on both classical and Christian topics. Sophronius, a scholarly patriarch of Jerusalem, composed a cycle of poems on the festivals of the Church year in the meters of classical Greek odes.

In Constantinople, scholarly members of the court and of the legal profession wrote epigrams in the classical Greek manner on pagan themes—the subjects were sometimes quite pagan indeed—and Paul the Silentiary, a functionary of the court, wrote a description of the new Church of St. Sophia in elegant Homeric verse. Procopius, in his histories, imitated the style of Herodotus and Thucydides. The reign has been called the golden age of Byzantine literature.

Justinian encouraged all these activities, for he understood the political as well as the literary and intellectual value of preservation of the Greek national heritage. This is the context in which occurred the famous action of the emperor in "closing" the philosophical schools of Athens in 529, the year in which he began his campaign against heretics and non-Christians. Classical philosophy was still being taught at Athens by Neoplatonic philosophers who were not Christians. Justinian did not, as some critics of his policies have supposed, close the schools at Athens because classical philosophy was being taught there. Classical philosophy was being taught elsewhere at the same time, by Christian scholars. What concerned Justinian was that at Athens the instruction was not offered in a Christian context. The pagan teachers might corrupt the minds of Christian students; indeed schools taught by pagans were an anachronism. Justinian did not in fact simply order the schools to be closed. The evidence indicates that he offered the teachers the opportunity to continue their work if they would become Christians. They declined, and departed as exiles to the court of the king of Persia, an enlightened monarch interested in scholarship. The schools then closed, and the instruction at Gaza, Alexandria, and elsewhere seems to have been sufficient for the demand.

The early Christian apologist Tertullian, expressing in memorable terms the hatred and fear that many early believers felt toward pagan learning and culture, had asked the famous question "What is there in common between Athens and Jerusalem? What between the Academy and the Church? What between heretics and Christians?" Justinian's vision was to bring together Athens and Jerusalem in Constantinople. It was not an accident that in classical Athens, the city that had epitomized Hellenic civilization, the principal shrine was the Parthenon, the temple of Athena, goddess of wisdom, and that in Constantinople the principal shrine was the church dedicated to St. Sophia, the Holy Wisdom of God. The civilization of Athens and the civilization of Jerusalem each represented a particular form of what was believed to be the truth, and Justinian saw as his task the completion of the process of adding the best parts of the truth of Athens to the higher truth of Jerusalem. Thus would be produced a civilization, represented in Constantinople, that would be the full expression of the life of the Christian Greco-Roman Empire.

• *Justinian and the Late Roman Empire* Justinian's reign was a failure in important ways. His wars of reconquest depleted the resources of the empire in men and wealth; the reconquered provinces were a drain rather than a source of support, and eventually it was not possible to keep possession of them. He failed in an ill-considered personal effort to bring peace in the Monophysite controversy. He allowed the army to fall dangerously below its proper footing, and his policies were so unpopular that there were plots to assassinate him in 548 and 562.

At the same time he established very clearly, and much more forcefully than his immediate predecessors had been able to do, a powerful conception of the role of the Roman

Empire in the world and of the role of the emperor in the
rule of the empire. His ideas were based on the history of
the empire and the history of the Church. He had a clear
awareness of the presentness of the past, that is, of the
present activity of the forces of past history and experience.
The continuity of experience, Justinian (and others) believed, would shape the future and assure the continuity of
Roman rule and Christian religion. To the future of
Roman rule he furnished a new instrument in the codification of the law—Justinian's unique contribution to the
preservation and transmission of the body of legal tradition
that was both a foundation of the empire and one of
Rome's greatest gifts to civilization.

In the same way Justinian, the heir of both Augustus and
Constantine, made his own individual contribution to the
symbiosis of Church and state. As a student of Roman history and legal institutions, Justinian had a very precise idea
of the nature of *imperium*, and as both a religious person
and an experienced administrator, he understood the nature of *sacerdotium*, in both its legal and its spiritual aspects. For the sake of his own responsibility, he brought
sacerdotium and *imperium* together with a clarity of definition and a forcefulness of action that left a lasting mark on
the imperial office—though it did not leave the same kind
of lasting mark on the Church since the Church, while in
given historical circumstances it necessarily finds itself active in a particular type of culture, is active in other types
as well and maintains its essentials in each type of worldly
civilization to which it belongs.

• *The Late Roman Empire and the Middle Ages, East
and West* But at the same time Justinian's reign illustrates
one of the problems with which scholars today have been
concerned, namely the reason or reasons why the Roman
state in the East continued to prosper after Roman power
in the West collapsed, half a century before Justinian's accession.

It is necessary to understand in the first place that the separation of East and West, in the latter part of the fifth century, was one stage in an ultimate division of two different kinds of civilization, Greek and Roman, that had been brought together by historical circumstances but had never become wholly integrated. The Roman conquest of the eastern Mediterranean in the Hellenistic period had produced a Roman Empire with a substantial Greek component, but Greek East and Latin West were never wholly assimilated and could not have been. The temperamental and intellectual differences between Greek and Roman could never be overcome, and the division between the eastern and western branches of the Church in the Byzantine Empire reflected a breach that was not wholly theological.

Before the time of the Late Roman Empire, the Roman state had given to the Greek East its political and material security, which provided for the preservation of the intellectual tradition of the Greek lands. The old Greek cities of the East, such as Athens, Antioch, and Alexandria, continued to typify the special culture of the independent and self-sufficient Greek *polis*, which did not have a counterpart in the Latin cities of the West, all of which looked to Rome for their culture.

The continuing life of the Greek cities was more than a cultural survival. It meant that the eastern provinces of the empire preserved a form of social life and a historical tradition that were older than the Roman state. The Greek *polis* was the essential unit on which the empire, in its eastern half, was built. The Hellenic tradition was an indigenous possession of the *polis*, something that Roman domination could not alter or take away. This tradition, preserved in the educational program of the *polis*, was a source of energy for the people of the Greco-Roman *polis* as it had been in the older *polis*. When the Greek cities became Greek Christian cities, they gained an added source of strength in their life as Christian communities.

Thus in the eastern empire the cities preserved a unity of religion and culture, under a stable central government, whereas the same conditions came to an end in the West. In the West, as the government collapsed, the Church became the recognized custodian of law and order and of intellectual culture. The popes continued to possess prestige and authority when the western emperors ruled as figureheads and eventually disappeared. In the West, the Church took over the custody of intellectual life when the cities, under barbarian occupation, ceased to be able to do so. The Rule of the Order of St. Benedict, established at Monte Cassino not far from Rome about 530 or 540, created, in a religious order, a form of intellectual community that in addition to its spiritual function preserved the scholarship of the classical tradition. The Rule organized each establishment of the order along the lines of a small city.

In the West, the monastery took the place of the city as the center of civilization; but no Monte Cassino was necessary in the East, where the cities were able to preserve their intellectual life. In the West, the Roman cities passed into the "dark ages," while Constantinople, as the brilliant symbol of classical and Christian culture and Roman rule, needed no more specific title than ancient Rome had needed, and could, like Rome, be known simply as "The City."

Table of Emperors and Events

West	*East*	
Maximian	Diocletian	301 Edict of Maximum Prices
C. 285–286	A. 284–305	
A. 286–305,		303–304 Edicts against Christians
307–310		
Constantius	Galerius	311 Galerius' edict of toleration
C. 293–305	C. 293–305	
A. 305–306	A. 305–311	
Constantine	Maximinus	
C. (305) 306–308	C. 305–308	
A. (306) 308–337	A. 308–313	
Severus		
A. 306–307		
Maxentius	Licinius	312 Battle of Milvian Bridge
A. 307–312	A. 308–324	312–313 Edicts of toleration of Constantine and Licinius
	Constantine	324 Battle of Chrysopolis; Foundation of Constantinople
	A. 324–337	325 Council of Nicaea
Constantine II		335 Outbreak of war with Persia
C. 317–337		
A. 337–340		
Constans	Constantius II	
C. 333–337	C. 324–337	
A. 337–350	A. 337–361	
Constantius II	Gallus	350–353 Usurpation of Magnentius in Gaul
A. 351–361	C. 350–354	
Julian	Julian	360 Julian proclaimed A. by his troops
C. 355–360	A. 361–363	
A. 360–363		
Jovian	Jovian	363 Treaty of peace with Persia
A. 363–364	A. 363–364	
Valentinian I	Valens	374 Ambrose elected bishop of Milan
A. 364–375	A. 364–378	
		378 Battle of Adrianople
Gratian	Theodosius I	381 Edicts on orthodoxy and against paganism; Council of Constantinople
A. 375–383	A. 379–395	
		382 Second edict on orthodoxy
Valentinian II		382–383 Controversy over Altar of Victory in Rome
A. 383–392		
		388 Massacre at Callinicum
Theodosius I		390 Massacre at Thessalonica; penance of Theodosius I
A. 394–395		

West	East	
	West *East*	
Honorius A. 395–423	Arcadius A. 395–408	395 Division of empire into East and West
		399 Massacre of Goths in Constantinople
	Theodosius II A. 408–450	408 Fall of Stilicho
		410 Alaric captures Rome
Valentinian III A. 425–455		425 Foundation of university of of Constantinople
		431 Council of Ephesus
		438 Publication of Code of Theodosius
		449 Second Council of Ephesus
	Marcian A. 450–457	451 Council of Chalcedon
		452 Huns invade Italy
Petronius Maximus A. 455		455 Vandals sack Rome
Avitus A. 455–456		
Majorian A. 457–461	Leo I A. 457–474	
Libius Severus A. 461–465		
Anthemius A. 467–472		
Olybrius A. 472		
Glycerius A. 473		
Julius Nepos A. 473		
Romulus A. 475–476	Leo II A. 474	476 End of Roman rule in Italy; Odoacer king in Italy
	Zeno A. 474–491	482 *Henotikon* of Zeno
		484–519 Schism between Rome and Constantinople
	Anastasius A. 491–518	502 Persia begins war
	Justin I A. 518–527	519 End of schism between Rome and Constantinople
	Justinian A. 527–565	529 Publication of first edition of Code of Justinian; persecution of heretics and

Bibliographical Note

Sources in translation may be found conveniently in the "Loeb Classical Library" (Cambridge, Mass.: Harvard University Press), in the "Select Library of Nicene and Post-Nicene Fathers," First and Second Series (reprinted by Wm. B. Eerdmans Publishing Co., Grand Rapids, Mich.), in the two series "Ancient Christian Writers" and "Fathers of the Church" (Washington: Catholic University of America Press), and in "Sources chrétiennes" (Paris: Les Éditions du Cerf). Other collections of translations on special subjects are mentioned below.

The best general survey of the history and institutions of the Late Roman Empire is the detailed and authoritative study by A. H. M. Jones, *The Later Roman Empire, 284–602: A Social, Economic and Administrative Survey*. The English edition (Oxford: Basil Blackwell & Mott Ltd., 1964) is in three volumes with folder of maps; the American edition (Norman, Okla.: University of Oklahoma Press, 1964) is in two volumes. This work includes an exhaustive list of the sources, but does not give a history of the literature of the period. The author has provided a shortened version in one volume: *The Decline of the Ancient World* (New York: Holt, Rinehart and Winston, Inc., 1966), which is the first volume of the series "A General History of Europe," edited by Denys Hay; it contains an introductory chapter on the sources. Written on a different plan, and designed to take less account of the history of institutions, is Ernest Stein, *Histoire du Bas-Empire*, edited by Jean-Rémy Palanque, 2 vols. (Paris-Brussels-Amsterdam: Desclée de Brouwer, 1949–1959); this covers the period 284–565. The work of Edward Gibbon, *The History of the Decline and Fall of the Roman Empire*, originally published in London in 1776–1788 (to be read in the edition of J. B. Bury, 7 vols., London, 1897–1902), though now superseded as a comprehensive account and reference work, still possesses importance because of the author's grasp of the fundamental significance of the continuity of the Roman state from the reign of Augustus to the fall of Constantinople in 1453. Gibbon's work possesses the further distinction, not often achieved by modern histories, of being a monument of English prose.

The foregoing comprehensive treatments are supplemented by histories devoted to special periods. In chronological order, the first that may be mentioned is Roger Rémondon, *La Crise de l'empire romain, de Marc-Aurèle à Anastase* (Paris: Presses Universitaires de France, 1964). A judicious account of the conversion of Constantine and of his reign has been written by A. H. M. Jones, *Constantine and the Conversion of Europe*, rev. ed. (New York: Collier Books, 1962; first published 1948). This contains a "Note on Books." For the period of the remainder of the fourth century, beginning with the reign of Constantine as sole emperor, André Piganiol, *L'Empire chrétien, 325–395* (in the series Histoire générale fondée per G. Glotz, Histoire romaine, IV, 2e partie; Paris: Presses Universitaires de France, 1947) is authoritative. The following period is covered by J. B. Bury, *History of the Later Roman Empire from the Death of Theodosius I to the Death of Justinian, A.D. 395 to A.D. 565*, 2 vols. (New York: Dover Publications, Inc., 1958; originally published 1923), a work important at the time of its publication and still readable, though it has now been replaced by the works of Jones and Stein. A thoughtful and well-illustrated account has been published by Joseph Vogt, *The Decline of Rome*, Eng. tr. (New York: New American Library of World Literature, Inc., 1967). Valuable insights into the history of the West leading up to the end of Roman rule are provided by Samuel Dill, *Roman Society in the Last Century of the Western Empire* (New York: Meridian Books, Inc., 1958; first published 1898).

The period of Justin I and Justinian is treated by A. A. Vasiliev, *Justin the First: An Introduction to the Epoch of Justinian the Great* (Cambridge, Mass.: Harvard University Press, 1950) and by Berthold Rubin, *Das Zeitalter Iustinians*, of which the first volume of a projected three-volume study has appeared (Berlin: De Gruyter, 1960). Less ambitious than Rubin's work but readable and useful is the treatment of John W. Barker, *Justinian and the Later Roman Empire* (Madison: University of Wisconsin Press, 1966), which has the merit of setting the reign of Justinian in the context of the preceding and following periods. Barker's book contains a useful bibliography. A brief study by G. Downey, *Justinian and the Imperial Office*, has been privately published by the University of Cincinnati (1968). The histories of Justinian's reign may be supplemented by several of the works cited below among the works on law and on art and architecture.

For the period of the barbarian invasion, we have a new critical study by Lucien Musset, *Les Invasions: les vagues germaniques* (Paris: Presses Universitaires de France, 1965), with which may be used a collection of texts in translation edited by C. D. Gordon, *The Age of Attila: Fifth-Century Byzantium and the Barbarians* (Ann Arbor: University of Michigan Press, 1960).

In addition to the histories listed above, every student of the period should be familiar with the essays and important review-articles of one of the most distinguished authorities on this period, Norman H. Baynes, collected in his *Byzantine Studies and Other Essays* (London: Athlone Press, University of London, 1955). Important insights into the period are also offered in the introduction by Baynes and chapters by various scholars in *Byzantium: An Introduction to East Roman Civilization,* edited by Baynes and H. St. L. B. Moss (Oxford: Clarendon Press, 1948; reprinted in Galaxy Books).

An important study of the social structure of the Roman Empire, which includes the period of the Late Empire, has been written by Jean Gagé, *Les Classes sociales dans l'empire romain* (Paris: Payot, 1964).

For the sources and development of political theory, which exerted such an important influence on the history of the Late Roman Empire, we now have the authoritative study of Francis Dvornik, *Early Christian and Byzantine Political Philosophy: Origins and Background,* 2 vols. (Washington: Dumbarton Oaks Research Library and Collection, 1966). For the government and administration of the empire in this period, there is an excellent basic account by Wilhelm Ensslin, "The Government and Administration of the Byzantine Empire" in the new edition of the *Cambridge Mediaeval History,* IV, pt. 2 (London: Cambridge University Press, 1967), pp. 1–54. Some important political texts of the period may be found in *Social and Political Thought in Byzantium from Justinian I to the Last Palaeologus: Passages from Byzantine Writers and Documents,* translated and edited by Ernest Barker (Oxford: Clarendon Press, 1957). The inscriptions and the imperial portraits on the coins provide valuable evidence for imperial policies; though some of the coins of the fourth century have not yet been published in adequate catalogues, we possess two resources in P. V. Hill, J. P. C. Kent, and R. A. G. Carson, *Late Roman Bronze Coinage, A.D. 324–498* (London: Spink and Son, 1965) and Warwick Wroth, *Imperial Byzantine Coins in the British Museum,* 2 vols. (London: British Museum, 1908; reprinted Chicago: Argonaut, 1966). Wroth's work covers the period 491–1453.

For an introduction to Roman law in the period of the Late Roman Empire, the best guide is H. F. Jolowicz, *Historical Introduction to the Study of Roman Law,* 2d ed. (London: Cambridge University Press, 1954). Several collections of legal texts and inscriptions in translation are available: *Ancient Roman Statutes,* edited and translated by A. C. Johnson, P. R. Coleman-Norton, and Frank C. Bourne (Austin: University of Texas Press, 1961); *The Theodosian Code and Novels and the Sirmondian Constitutions,* edited and translated by Clyde Pharr and others (Princeton, N.J.: Princeton University Press, 1952); *Justinian, Digest,* translated by C. H. Monro, 2 vols. (London: Cambridge University Press, 1904–1909); and *The Institutes of Justinian,* translated by J. B. Moyle, 5th ed. (Oxford: Clarendon Press, 1913). *The Civil Law,* translated by S. P. Scott (Cincinnati: Central Trust Co., 1932), is inaccurate.

Histories of the Church during the period of the Late Roman Empire are numerous. Two collections of basic documents in translation have been edited by J. Stevenson: *A New Eusebius: Documents Illustrative of the History of the Church to A.D. 337* (London: S. P. C. K., 1957) and *Creeds, Councils and Controversies: Documents Illustrative of the History of the Church, A.D. 337–461* (London: S. P. C. K., 1966). The best brief introduction to the Church and Christian culture in the Late Roman Empire is J. W. C. Wand, *Doctors and Councils* (London: Faith Press, 1962), which deals with the Greek and Latin Fathers of the Church and the councils from Nicaea through Chalcedon. Brief introductions to Church history during this period are W. H. C. Frend, *The Early Church* (Philadelphia: J. P. Lippincott Company, 1966) and Henry Chadwick, *The Early Church* (Baltimore: Penguin Books, Inc., 1967; The Pelican History of the Church, vol. 1). On a larger scale is Hans Lietzmann, *A History of the Early Church,* vols. 3–4, Eng. tr. (London: Lutterworth Press, 1953), reprinted in one volume by Meridian Books, Inc. (New

York, 1961). These volumes cover the period to about A.D. 400. A detailed history of the Church during the period A.D. 313–461 is B. J. Kidd, *A History of the Church at A.D. 461*, vols. 2–3 (Oxford: Clarendon Press, 1922). A valuable account of the latter part of the period is provided by George Every, *The Byzantine Patriarchate, 451–1204*, 2d ed. (London: S. P. C. K., 1962). On monasticism, see D. J. Chitty, *The Desert a City: An Introduction to the Study of Egyptian and Palestinian Monasticism under the Christian Empire* (Oxford: Basil Blackwell & Mott Ltd., 1966).

For an introductory study of the relationships between Christianity and the Roman state, see T. M. Parker, *Christianity and the State in the Light of History* (London: A. & C. Black Ltd., 1955), and, on a larger scale, the work of F. Dvornik cited above. A special study of an important phase of the relationship is the monograph of Noel Q. King, *The Emperor Theodosius and the Establishment of Christianity* (Philadelphia: The Westminster Press, 1960). A pioneer study still of value is E. L. Woodward, *Christianity and Nationalism in the Later Roman Empire* (London: Longmans, Green & Co., Ltd., 1916). *Roman State and Christian Church: A Collection of Legal Documents to A.D. 533*, edited and translated by P. R. Coleman-Norton, 3 vols. (London: S. P. C. K., 1966) is to be used with caution since the material is not presented completely.

Among the accounts of the interaction of Christianity and paganism and the emergence of Christian culture may be mentioned C. N. Cochrane, *Christianity and Classical Culture: A Study of Thought and Action from Augustus to Augustine*, rev. ed. (New York: Oxford University Press, 1944; reprinted in Galaxy Books). One of the best treatments of the theme is the last published work of Werner Jaeger, *Early Christianity and Greek Paideia* (Cambridge, Mass.: Harvard University Press, 1961). The basic study by H. O. Taylor, *The Emergence of Christian Culture in the West: The Classical Heritage of the Middle Ages* (New York: Harper & Row, Publishers, 1958; originally published 1911) has an important foreword and bibliography by K. M. Setton. A collection of lectures by various scholars delivered at the Warburg Institute, London, in 1958–1959 has been edited by A. Momigliano, *The Conflict between Paganism and Christianity in the Fourth Century* (Oxford: Clarendon Press, 1963).

Among the numerous treatments of art and architecture in the

Late Roman Empire may be mentioned D. Talbot Rice, *The Beginnings of Christian Art* (Nashville: Abingdon Press, 1958); Michael Gough, *The Early Christians* (New York: Frederick A. Praeger, Inc., 1961); Jean Lassus, *The Eary Christian and Byzantine World*, Eng. tr. (New York: McGraw-Hill, Inc., 1967); William L. MacDonald, *Early Christian and Byzantine Architecture* (New York: George Braziller, Inc., 1962); W. F. Volbach and M. Hirmer, *Early Christian Art* (London: Thames and Hudson, Ltd., 1961); André Grabar, *Byzantine Painting* (Cleveland: The World Publishing Company, 1953); the same scholar's *The Golden Age of Justinian*, edited by A. Malraux and G. Salles, Eng. tr. (New York: Golden Press, Inc., 1967); John Beckwith, *The Art of Constantinople* (New York: Phaidon Publishers, Inc., 1961); D. Talbot Rice, *Constantinople* (New York: Stein and Day, 1965); Gervase Mathew, *Byzantine Aesthetics* (London: John Murray, 1963). Of special interest are two studies of the history of art in relation to political life: H. P. L'Orange, *Art Forms and Civic Life in the Late Roman Empire* (Princeton, N.J.: Princeton University Press, 1965, a translation of *Fra Principat til Dominat*, 1958), dealing with the period of the Tetrarchy and Constantine; and André Grabar, *L'Empereur dans l'art byzantin: Recherches sur l'art officiel de l'empire d'Orient* (Paris: Les Belles Lettres, 1936). An important collection of antiquities of this period is expertly described and illustrated by M. C. Ross, *Catalogue of the Byzantine and Early Medieval Antiquities in the Dumbarton Oaks Collection*, 2 vols. (Washington: Dumbarton Oaks Research Library and Collection, 1962–1965).

The importance of the roles of the Greek cities in the history of the period is shown by the comprehensive works of A. H. M. Jones, *The Cities of the Eastern Roman Provinces* (Oxford: Clarendon Press, 1937; new edition in preparation) and *The Greek City from Alexander to Justinian* (Oxford: Clarendon Press, 1940). On Antioch at this period, on which we possess a good bit of information, see Paul Petit, *Libanius et la vie municipale à Antioche au IVᵉ siècle après J.-C.* (Paris: Geuthner, 1955) and G. Downey, *Ancient Antioch* (Princeton, N.J.: Princeton University Press, 1962). A series of three studies by G. Downey deals with three of the cities at periods when they were at the height of their influence on the history and culture of the Late Roman Empire: *Antioch in the Age of Theodosius the Great*

(1962), *Gaza in the Early Sixth Century* (1963), and *Constan-tinople in the Age of Justinian* (second printing with revisions, 1968), all published at Norman by the University of Oklahoma Press.

On the important and difficult subject of the decline of Roman power in the West, only the most significant of a number of studies can be mentioned in a limited space; most of the works cited contain bibliographies. The best pronouncements on the subject are those of Baynes in his *Byzantine Studies and Other Essays* (cited above) and of A. H. M. Jones in the concluding chapter of his *Later Roman Empire* (cited above). Collections of the opinions of modern scholars, reprinted from various sources, are available in *The Fall of Rome: Can it be Explained?* edited by Mortimer Chambers (New York: Holt, Rinehart and Winston, Inc., 1964), and in the relevant chapters in *The De-cline of Empires,* edited by S. N. Eisenstadt (Englewood Cliffs, N.J.: Prentice-Hall, Inc., 1967). A collection (though not abso-lutely exhaustive) of theories that have been advanced may be found in the introduction to Ferdinand Lot, *The End of the Ancient World and the Beginnings of the Middle Ages,* Eng. tr. (New York: Harper & Row, Publishers, 1961), with introduction, additional notes, and additional bibliography by G. Downey. A study from a fresh point of view has been made by W. C. Bark, *Origins of the Medieval World* (Stanford, Calif.: Stanford University Press, 1958). A new study of special interest by Walter E. Kaegi, Jr., *Byzantium and the Decline of Rome* (Princeton, N.J.: Princeton University Press, 1968) deals with the reactions in the East to the decline of Roman power in the West.

Two excellent collections of maps which are easily accessible are those edited by Colin McEvedy, *The Penguin Atlas of An-cient History* (Baltimore: Penguin Books, Inc., 1967), which covers the period to A.D. 362, and *The Penguin Atlas of Medieval History* (Baltimore: Penguin Books, Inc., 1961), which begins at A.D. 362. Excellent maps are provided by Jones, *The Later Roman Empire* (cited above); see also F. van der Meer, *Atlas of the Early Christian World* (London: Thomas Nelson & Sons, 1958).

Index